THE ROOTS IN A WOMAN

DISCOVERING AND UPROOTING THE WEEDS AND DEEP ROOTS THAT ENTANGLE OUR LIVES

PAIGE LOEHR

The Roots in a Woman:
Discovering and Uprooting the Weeds and Deep Roots that Entangle our Lives

Copyright © 2021 by Paige Loehr

Published by Common Ground.
All rights reserved.

CONTENTS

INTRODUCTION

Hello Darling, I am so glad that you have decided to join me on this journey of discovering some of the roots that can hide deep inside of you. As women, we tend to appear to the male species like we are crazy. Honestly, there is no woman I know that at least at one point has not been just that, a little crazy. I would even dare to say we are all truly just stark raving mad. What I think is, you are either a good crazy or a bad crazy. Good crazy to me means you are crazy confident, you're crazy fun, you're crazy radiant, and you're crazy good to the people in your life. And bad crazy is just that, all bad. For me, to uncover and uproot some of the deep dark things that lay inside was the key to shed the bad crazy and step into the good.

The fact is that we are wired differently than men. We FEEL differently. We think differently. I wanted all the depth that came with all of the feelings I have. The depth that I felt was helpful to me. And not just the good feelings, but some of the bad caused me to go further and learn more about myself. I don't know about you, but I didn't want to have to cut out my "feeler" to not appear like a lunatic to the people around me. I did not want to sweep everything under the rug in my life to avoid conflict because I felt like confronting my issues would only make me better. I knew that there was no way that everything I went through was in vain, but no lesson would be learned if I left well enough alone. When there seemed to be an invisible border holding me back, I knew it was time to make changes. I knew it was time to invest in the only weed eater to keep them from returning by attacking the root, God.

So, I went on a journey with God's word as my tool, and through the strength of the Holy Spirit, I began to be the gardener of my soul. I will not claim to have a green thumb seeing how I have killed many plants, but I know that God does. God has proven to keep anything alive and to make even barren places fruitful. As long as he was with me, no matter how much of an amateur gardener I was, I knew he would guide me.

I started to tackle the weeds first because they stood out and were just not pleasing to look at. These were the things that I felt were the easiest to see from the outside. Then God would direct me to this other plot of land in my life. In those moments, I felt Him telling me you can spend all day removing those weeds but over here are some big trees that are now dead. These 20-year old trees are rotting at their core, and they are spreading poison. Sure, what you are doing with those weeds will, on the surface, make things temporarily appear nice and manicured. The problem is they will just rise again. And no topical spray is going to help either.

God also began to point out the real danger that was present with these giant dead rotting trees. When a freeze comes, they will shatter and send the branches like shards of glass exploding through your life. If a wild wind storm blows through, they will fall right over and smash any of the work you try and do here in this garden. The enormous dead tree may not look too bad, so they are easy to ignore, but they threaten to lay waste to anything that you build here.

If I began planting now, I could very soon start to see some beauty arise in my life, but that beauty would be temporary, and the fleeting beauty that I could display would remain under the shadow of those dying trees. I would end up getting frustrated in a place of perpetual back and forth, and I would have had no idea why my life felt like it was one step ahead and then two steps back. Once God showed me that all the work I was doing to make things pretty in my life was pointless, I was willing to make real and lasting change. I was tired of going up and down on the roller coaster, and I just wanted to move forward. Finally, I would pinpoint what was causing the disease in my life, and I knew there was something there. I could feel the restriction but had never been able to find the roots. I realized that finding the root meant finding the source of what kept me from being free to produce for the kingdom of God. When I uprooted the entangling things, it meant the beauty I was planting would not turn to ash.

If that is where you find yourself, then get ready to change. I will talk to you in this book as if I was sitting across the table from you. On each of these topics, I am going to tell you bits and pieces of my story. I will tell you how God dealt with me on each subject and how he healed me in so many areas.

Most importantly, I will help guide you not only to the vast decaying trees in your life, but we are going to UPROOT THEM completely. We are not just knocking down the visible things in this book because that is easy enough for you to do independently. I am not talking to you about the things that everyone can see. I am talking to you as a friend about the items in your life that you have hidden. The stuff beneath the surface has spread through your body and infected your soul. We will dig and dig until we find every root anchored to the big dying trees in your life. We will cut away the pain and the darkness that always seems to shadow your life and cut out all of the rotten fruit at the very root.

It may be uncomfortable, and I am almost guaranteeing that. But remember, I am here with you. We are in the quiet corner of a coffee shop, where it is ok to shed some tears. Between sips of coffee and pounded keys on my MacBook, I, too, have shed tears while writing this. Know this, my friend, that I am not some educated person trying to fix you with my knowledge. I am a healed person trying to help you through the power of my testimony.

I am not a doctor, a therapist, a psychology major with a Master's degree in fixing your problems. I am only high school educated with a doctorate in seeking the presence of a Holy God that is capable of knocking down every stronghold and ripping out every root inside of you. I am coming to you as a sister, telling you the cool story of what our dad has done for me in hopes that we can go to him together into his word and through prayer to receive the same things for you.

He is not a respecter of persons, the gifts, blessings, and all of the uprootings he has done for me. He is more than willing to do for you if you will allow him to.

You do have to promise not to judge me. I am going to open my heart and my past and the pain that was there. I will tell you about things that I have done that I am not proud of, if only you promise to be gentle with me.

So come, sit down with me and let's have a chat. Get yourself comfortable but not too comfortable because you will have to get dirty. You may have to throw on your mom's old gardening gloves or buy a new pair from Target, and I'm sure they have some attractive options.

Holy Father, I thank you right now for this Dear sister who has chosen to come on this journey with me. I ask right now that you soften her heart and allow her to open up to the words that are in this book. I feel like I have operated in obedience to you and that these words here are Holy Spirit inspired, but they still carry no weight unless your presence comes with them. So let this be a journey that we take together, me, my new friend, and most importantly, your presence God. We need you to uproot the things in our lives that keep us from the fruitful lives we know that we can have when living in your fullness. We are ready for you to do work in us right now, and we thank you for being willing. We are prepared for FREEDOM in you.

Alright, sister, Let's do this.

1

BITTER ROOT

Never trust your tongue when your heart is bitter. Be better,
not bitter.

Ladies, this one is going to hurt, but it's for your own good.
Think of it as a hair removal process on the upper lip or
chin where there just shouldn't be hair. You know that it will
hurt to get it gone, but you are willing to do it because of how
unsightly it is. Trust me, girl, that bitter root you got there is even
nastier.

In most cases, the ugly truth is that we love our bitter roots.
Regardless of how nasty it makes us feel, we keep it because if
we let go, it is as if it dismisses the wrong done to us. Maybe we
aren't ready to let go of that pain. I mean, that person hurt you,
you were disappointed, they betrayed you and broke your heart.

Not being ready to let go doesn't mean that you are not
prepared to release the pain. I believe that it means you are not
ready to release the person of the pain they have caused you. To
let go, maybe you feel there is some step that needs to be taken,

someway this wrong needs to be made right. So what if this never happens in the way you feel you need it to at this moment. Will you remain in bondage.

In this life, there is no shortage of pain. There is no doubt that the cuts that go deepest come from those you thought would never hurt you. So let's dive into the bitterness that nestles deep in you towards someone that has done you wrong.

Sometimes the worst hurts can be when the one who caused it hasn't even acknowledged that they were wrong or apologized because they remain clueless or they just don't care. Maybe they did apologize, and it just didn't seem genuine or sufficient enough for how awful they made you feel. Or if you are anything like me, then sorry is just not enough when I cannot sense or see any real change. If there was no change, then my assumption was always that it would only happen again.

I have been there, and I know how poisonous it can be to let all of that rot on the inside. There are all of these scriptures about forgiving so that you, yourself, can be forgiven. I have read them all in a relentless search to find out how. After several failed attempts, regardless of how hard I tried, I couldn't get past this remaining wound that seemed too deep to remove.

Have you ever tried to forgive, but you get angry and resentful every time you think of your unjust treatment? You even try to be around them, and with one word or action not even geared towards you, your thoughts of the past are triggered, and you are annoyed all over again. The turmoil you were subjected to in the past begins spending around you until it sucks you in.

Sometimes people have a hard time identifying deeper issues like this, and they justify their reactions and emotions in that specific situation. That has been me in the past. Instead of realizing that my history with this person is clouding my current judgment, I try to justify why in that situation, my perspective is correct.

Well, let's look at the definition and maybe not take it so deeply.

Bitter: angry, hurt, or resentful because of one's bad experiences or a sense of unjust treatment. Having a sharp, pungent taste or smell; not sweet.

When I read this definition, I finally had clarity with why I was feeling the way that I was.

So let me ask you this when you are around this person does your mood tend to turn sour? Are they to you like a pungent and sharp smell that is a nuisance?

If this is your response, let me just apply the hot wax and tell you.... You are BITTER!

Don't you want to get BETTER?

Hebrews 12:15 "See to it that no one comes short of the Grace of God; that no root of bitterness springing up causes trouble, and by it, many are defiled."

When you genuinely want to forgive, more needs to be done than just saying to yourself or that person, "I forgive you." You have to extend grace, which is a covering of all sin. No matter the unjust thing they did, you extend them that grace which says that you are human and to err is human.

The hard pill to swallow is that the sins of your life are no worse than theirs, and in some cases, that seems impossible. Even looking at someone with judgment can cause as much damage as physical abuse could cause another. So the challenge is not only to forgive the person but recognize what they did as a mistake (whether they know it or not), and you choose to smear grace all over it. This action keeps you from letting bitterness take root. You're not saying, "I forgive you but what you did was wrong" because even then, it is still taking root. You're saying, "I forgive you. I know you had no idea how much pain your actions would cause me, so I am letting go of all that. The pain and the resentment."

Listen, every person still has to have their day to answer to God for the things they have done. For me, the reason I wanted to hold on to others' discrepancies was that I felt I could find a way to punish them. If I let go, I thought they would get let off the hook. I completely forgot that I am not the judge, the jury, or the executioner in these cases. So why let what they did to you continue its work of defiling you on the inside because you are not willing to put on your gardening gloves and pull up the root. Even if this means that they aren't held accountable, at least their sins will no longer be blemishes on your heart. Our scripture says that bitterness causes trouble and defiles many.

Defile: Sully, Mar, or Spoil.
—desecrate or profane (something sacred)
—violate the purity of a woman.

How ugly is the word defile? It was chosen and placed in the scripture for a reason. Let me dig a little bit deeper, my darling, to help paint a picture. A person could have gone as far as to have abused you sexually, but when you let it take root, you also let them ravage your heart and soul. Don't you dare give them that power, dear girl. I know you want the plague of bitterness to go. It's bad enough it had the chance to get placed there, to begin with. When it lingers there, you just relive it over and over again, being mentally and emotionally defiled on repeat. It's like cancer on the inside of you, no one can see it, but it is killing you.

I have had my fair share of bitterness. I had roots in my life from my childhood and feeling abandoned by my father. So when the offense took root for how someone treated me, not only were they punished for their actions, they would be getting the punishment for my Dad's actions as well. In my mind, I could not comprehend how someone could be so unaware of the fact that they were causing you pain. I just assumed that everything that hurt me was intentional. So when you intentionally hurt someone, you deserve the punishment that comes along with it. If you knew me in the past, then you know that I could be pretty ruthless, so if you found your way to my crazy side, you were going to feel my wrath. I would intimidate and diminish people with just the way I ignored them, and it was deeper than the childhood game of the silent treatment. I took it way too far.

The problem with all of this is that it is far more hurtful to you and your soul to hold on to such anger, such hate, and behave in this manner. You end up putting so much thought into how you are treating a person, and if you are inflicting them with enough pain, you are not even able to enjoy your life, and moments are forever stolen from you.

At some point, I just realized I was not always going to get from people what I wanted, not a confession, not an apology, and sometimes no change to their behavior. I also realized that the way I was behaving was not going to help. I realized if I was to be Free, it was up to me to let God deal with that pain. I did not want my freedom to be pending on someone else changing. It wasn't as easy as a moment of prayer where I just said I forgive. I had to put work into completely letting go of that pain. I had to tell myself I would trust God to handle it, and I even had to pray for the person. I know to you that it may seem like a punishment worse than death to have to pray for someone that hurt you, but when you do that, the power they have over your life is released. Over time you will even have the hate you once felt removed entirely. You cannot hate someone that you pray for. So I ask you, sis, do you want to be Free?

Okay, I think it's time now. The wax pot is hot. Let's get it in place and let it rip.

Ok, on the count of 3!

1, 2, 3

NOW LETS UPROOT!

You are now the Gardener, so dig deeper. Remember we are sitting across the table from each other, so talk to me. Tell me the bitterness that plagues you. Tell me all about what happened and get it all out right now here in this moment.

Journal

What are the painful events that took place in your life that still plague you today?

Do you feel like you are truly ready to let go?

Can you trust God to handle the situation for you?

How do you plan to stay free of this bitterness?

Take Action

- Pray today for someone who has hurt you.
- Declare your forgiveness (in some cases, this was just something I did alone, but sometimes I felt God calling me to tell the person that I forgive them)
- That is between you and God. Listen, he will guide you.
- God, will you speak to me and help me stay Free.....
- Ask God for his perspective, and he may show you something you didn't see before (hurting people, hurt people).

Prayer

Right now, in the name of Jesus, by his power and authority, I speak to all residue of bitterness inside of me, and I say UPROOT! This negativity and this poison are no longer welcome. This is your final eviction notice. You must vacate with all of your belongings immediately. I speak for every empty place that has now been made available to be filled with God's grace, his healing, and his love. That there be no place left vacant for that bitterness to return. I am FREE of the pain of that incident, and I am now entirely FREE to forgive. Thank you, Jesus.

Here is one disclaimer that can maybe help keep you Free. Just because you have forgiven someone and removed the bitterness does not mean that you have to have a relationship with that person. Or you may want the relationship to be restored. And if that is the case, I believe it can be. You may have a situation where restoration just won't work, and there is nothing wrong with that. True forgiveness is not based on a relationship returning to where it once was. The important thing is that you are no longer holding on to all of the pain, and you've thrown away that old bitter root.

2

COMPARISON

Compare: estimate, measure, or note the similarity or dissimilarity between.

"A comparison is an act of violence against the self."—Iyanla Vanzant

This topic can almost be second nature to most women. I think it starts as a healthy curiosity. You're a young child, and you meet other kids, and they are different from you. So you look at them quizzically up and down, then you look back at yourself and compare. At first, it doesn't matter to you, but the older you get, the more you compare and begin to see yourself as less than. This is because whatever you perceive as good in someone else, something you may be lacking or you are the opposite of, you assume that your version is terrible. My friend has the cutest little feet, and mine are massive, ugh, which must mean mine are ugly. You see how simple it is in our minds to conclude, and it's just improper deductive reasoning.

I remember watching a show when I was young called Corina Corina. In the movie, two little girls were friends. One was black, and one was white. The girls in the movie obviously could tell there was a difference, and it was not bad. It just sparked curiosity. So in the film, they each have a lick of each other's arm to see if skin color tastes like the flavor related. You know that skin doesn't taste like flavors, so you know what results they found. The funny thing is that women grow up to remain that curious about each other, but it's more than just finding out your friends' flavor. It's about the fact that once you do, you begin to think yours couldn't possibly taste as good as theirs because it is different.

Maybe you see that your friend is excelling in Math, and that subject just doesn't click like that for you, and you make that comparison. For whatever reasoning that goes through our minds, that brings you to the conclusion that you aren't as smart as her. You completely fail to realize that her grades in English are never quite what yours seem to be. You have no idea that she will become an architect and you will become a writer. If you had such incredible hindsight, life would be so much easier.

One of my first memories of comparison was me with my cousin Chelsey. She is my cousin on my dad's side. We were both mixed but with different things. I am black/white, and she is black/white & Filipino. The one distinct thing about her I just couldn't help but compare to is that her hair was dark, straight, and shiny. Here I was with crazy curly dirty blonde hair, and it just didn't seem to shine like hers. Because of comparison and the fact that I thought her hair was so pretty, and mine was so different, I thought then that mine was ugly. I guess it just never really crossed my mind that both could be lovely, only in their way. The most ironic thing is that I recently found out that my cousin felt the same way I did when we were young. We met for dinner, and her hair wasn't iron curled, so I asked her how she did it, and she said she had gotten it permed. She said she had always wanted curly hair like mine. How silly are we?

We are going to go through the rest of our lives encountering people that are different than us. To not observe this would mean you would have to shut people out, which is just not feasible or healthy. We have to realize that everyone is different, but no one is better. If you look, think, or act differently from another person, that doesn't mean that you are flawed in some way, so don't even go down that thought pattern. You have to learn to compare notes, take what is useful from each and realize that it is just that much better when you combine the two. That is what every relationship and friendship should be, a celebration of the differences among you. It doesn't even hurt to acknowledge that you admire what someone else may have that you don't, but you mustn't compare and then judge yourself. Most importantly, you must not try to become someone that you are not. Growing and changing are great, but not to become a carbon copy of another.

You can see another person's beauty, brains, wit and enjoy it, but just don't get in the habit of getting out your measuring tools and begin to try and decipher which is more significant. No matter what you may estimate as far as value goes, you are wrong unless it is equal. Each of us is worth the same to God, and that worth is far beyond anything we could ever try and calculate.

Galatians 6:4-5 Each of you must examine your actions. Then you can be proud of your accomplishments without comparing yourself to others. Assume your responsibility.

When we read scripture, we tend to separate it too much, and when we do that, we disconnect things that are meant to go hand in hand. Here it says that we are to examine our actions, and then in the next sentence, it says that when you do that, you can be proud of your accomplishments without comparing yourself to others.

When you truly take the time to look at yourself, who you are, what you are good at, what you have that is unique to you, then you will know just how simply amazing you are. It's ok, don't feel as though this makes you selfish or proud. That is just not the case. It just means that you have created yourself aware of your value. When you know how much you are worth, once you fully embrace this truth that God gave you talents and abilities that, if used, will cause you to excel. Then you will, like the scripture says, beam with pride. At that moment, when you have dove into your gifts, you will take way less notice of the talents and abilities that were bestowed upon others that may be absent to you. What does it matter what so and so can say or do or be? You are fully equipped to become the person you aim to be, and you lack nothing.

How cool would it be if we were all able to live knowing our worth? To also be proud of your accomplishments as well as your unique characteristics without being self-conscious? What if the people that surrounded you were able to live in the same manner? What a different world we would live in. It is your responsibility to be that person and to set that example. If you choose to be unapologetically you, and then it will be contagious to those around you. Then all the comparisons that people live with making every day will become a thing of the past. Though this notion may seem naive, I know that you could at the very least inspire your sphere of influence to live this way. It is far more straightforward than we make it out to be. Once you have truly accepted how awesome you are, you will once again be able to witness your friends' differences and celebrate them without that causing you to question yourself. That type of woman is a scarce gem, and women like that have the power to shift things.

One other thing that I think is important for us all to consider when it comes to this topic is comparing the season of life you are into the season another is in. We often look at our life and feel as though we aren't where we should be, while others seem to be in the right spot in their lives. Let me caution you by saying this, and others may be in their winning season. It is important to remember that you don't know what they lost in their losing season. There are some people in their winning season. The truth is, I do not know all they lost in their losing season. And if I do not want to have to go through what they went through then, I shouldn't compare and desire their outcome. This mindset is helpful when I feel tempted to compare my life to someone else's.

What do you think Darling, would you like to be a trendsetter? Choosing to leave comparison behind you can indeed be a trailblazer that will bring true freedom to those around you.

Journal

How have you compared yourself in the past?

What do you feel causes you to compare yourself to others the most?

What about yourself have you been overlooking or not taking into consideration when you are making your comparisons?

Action Steps

- Make a list of things that make you unique (physical attributes).
- Make a list of your talents and abilities.
- Choose a friend that you have compared yourself to, celebrate her differences here, and then send her a text letting her know how awesome you think she is.

Prayer

Father, will you help me to get past my tendency to compare myself to others? Forgive me for, at times, not seeing the greatness that you created in me and weighing myself up against others. I ask that you help me better understand what I bring to the table, no matter how different they may be from everyone else. I just want to get to know myself better to see what you see and no longer focus on what you have given to others. You are perfect in all of your ways, and all you create is good, and I fall under that category. Help me each day to live in and acknowledge that truth. That comparison habit is now broken, and I am FREE to see me.

3

ABANDONMENT

Abandoned: Having been deserted or cast off. Unrestrained and uninhibited.

The most painful goodbyes are the ones that are never said and never explained.

It seems as though there is no limit to the things that we can endure in this life when we realize that God is with us. Let me just tell you right now, dear friend, that if you have suffered from even one of these roots and made it through, you are strong and capable of winning battles for the kingdom of heaven.

Being abandoned can be so difficult because you typically experience it in your childhood when there is so much about life that you do not yet understand. Then there are some cases when you have made it into your adult life, never having experienced it. So if it does happen, it leaves you feeling blindsided. Maybe it is a close friendship or in the marriage that you thought would be your happily ever after. Either way, it is not just a feeling that resides on the surface, but because of the nature of the pain that comes with it, it cuts deep and manifests itself in your core.

The feelings that come with being abandoned are so piercing that it is not something you only feel, but it tends to become a part of who you are. How you make decisions and how you form relationships going forward become dictated by this root. It is an ugly beast, and for the most part, it is because it preys upon the innocent and unsuspecting.

This feeling for me began in my youth. My dad's drug addiction caused him to be in and out of my life. He was never really there for my two older siblings and wasn't even present at their births, but it was during a season when he was trying when I was born. My mom and dad got married in Jamaica when there was suspicion that she was pregnant with me. They stayed together long enough for him to make it to my birth, and being there for that resulted in him trying to do right and stay. Unfortunately, that desire wasn't strong enough, though, when it came up against the demons of addiction. He did manage to stick around long enough, though, for me to form a bond with him.

My siblings had probably already begun dealing with the issues that came with being abandoned repeatedly. At the time, they were just waiting for him to leave again. I didn't know about all of that, and I just knew he was there, and I loved him. I don't know how long he managed to stay after I was born, but I was still a baby when he left for the first time. I have been thinking about it more lately than I ever had before for the simple reason that I am now a mother. My daughter is almost 2-years old, and I stay at home with her. My husband also works from home so that she can see both of us during the day.

I remember my daughter was six months old, and I noticed as she watched her dad stand up and walk into the kitchen. She waited, just staring in that general direction when he went out of sight until he came back into view, and she began to smile. I mentioned at that moment to my husband that I was probably about that age when my dad left for the first time. It made me sad to think about it because I realized that there might have been moments when I looked around to see where he was, and I couldn't find him. He specifically stood out because not only was he my dad, but he is black. I know that sounds funny, but my mom is white with red hair, and my siblings were like me with really dark hair. But I am sure my dad stood out and was distinct in my household. I wonder when that moment was for me when I watched him leave the room and waited patiently, and he didn't soon return.

I look at my daughter, and I couldn't even fathom having to be separated from her, especially not by my own doing. All of this made me realize that the seeds of abandonment begin when you start to notice that someone you had gotten used to and formed a relationship with is no longer there. For me, I was a baby. Those seeds were planted and continued to germinate throughout my childhood.

You know your story, and some may even have more dramatic cases. Maybe you were given up for adoption, and though the decision was an attempt to be selfless, it has left you feeling like a cast-off with a lack of understanding and some major identity issues. Sometimes we know that what happened was actually for the best, but that does not change how it makes you feel.

It is unreasonable to think that it can just go away without work. This is where I feel like so many people are naive. They just want to cover up their problems and build a strong foundation with God, all the while ignoring all of the things underneath the surface. It is hard to make something smooth and stable on a rocky foundation. It is hard to build on the rock when you have attempted to stack the rock on top of many tiny sharp pebbles. You can decide you want to start now with God and tackle your future, but you will not trust him and his guidance for your life if somewhere in there you have a lack of trust because at some point you felt like he had let you be abandoned. Or like me, you fear he too might choose to one day leave without explanation.

Some people blame God, and some people don't, but regardless of abandonment issues, it will be hard to follow the plan that God has for your life because it never entirely makes sense when you are taking your first steps. In those moments of starting on the path, you can tend to feel alone even though the truth is, you never were. So you have to work on that. You have to get down to that root and understand how it is affecting you.

What helped the most was to picture those memories when I was feeling the most deserted and left behind. I would also imagine God's heartbreaking. I would picture him hurting as he watched me wallow in that feeling. I would imagine him trying to whisper to me and get my attention because he indeed was so nearby. How hard was it for God to see me hurting, knowing he could make it all the better if I only knew that his presence would fill the void. When I pictured that moment in this way, I felt less alone and more loved.

Psalm 27:10 though my father and mother abandoned me, the Lord gathers me up. I love the way this scripture describes God dealing with abandonment. To gather something up indicates that it is scattered and isn't what happens to you when someone you love leaves. It is like they take a piece of you with them.

I began to let the Lord pick up the pieces that my father had left behind. There were parts of me that were thrown about every time I got off the bus, wondering if he would be home, and he wasn't. The pieces that were shattered every holiday and birthday that he didn't make an appearance for. The pieces left at the window the nights I watched for him because he told me he was coming and never showed up. The crushed pieces when he made me promises that were never fulfilled and when he chose things over me every day.

God picked up those pieces bit by bit because I could feel him draw near every time I called out to him. Every time I listened for God to speak, he spoke. Every single time I went to him with my heart, he returned to me with an answer. He picked up all of the pieces because he has never let me down, and he never will.

There were even those moments where things just didn't look the way they were supposed to in my mind's eye. I knew I was following the path that he was leading me down. I prayed, and it seemed as if at that moment he was choosing not to listen. I would begin to analyze myself, asking what I had done wrong like I did when I was a child. Why isn't he here? What could I have done better? Was I asking for too much? Was I annoying him? These tendencies came from the past and the questions that I asked myself when I would arrive at a once again fatherless home.

While trying my hardest to trust God, those insecurities would arise, and I would think maybe he has given up on me too. But then God would show up, and he would show off. No, not all of the times did it look how I had expected. It was always so much better and so much more than I could have asked for. When I was beginning to get impatient, he was just continuing to work things out on my behalf.

Ultimately, I think more than anything, God wants to know if we will lean into him and trust in those moments. Even though we may be whiny, at least we haven't sought out other things. Or are we going to accuse him of leaving us and try to seek out other means to be fulfilled? Are we going to make God suffer the consequences of the people in our lives that have abandoned us? Or are we going to choose to trust again in the promises spoken to us?

If I have done anything, it is just that I have chosen to take him at his word regardless of how many times words meant nothing, and they didn't equate to promises. I decided to believe that when God says something, it is a promise that will be fulfilled.

Hebrews 13:5 I will never leave thee nor forsake thee.

And I believe that with everything that I am, even when I don't feel it in moments, I just press in a little further, and he is always right there. I trust him, and I put my life in his hands, knowing that if I am in need, I seek Him first, and I put no other man in that position, and he is always faithful to respond.

Because of the trust I have in him, I can trade in my root of abandonment for a reckless abandonment in God. I can cast off worry, doubts, fears, pains, and all that may weigh me down and breathe in peace without concern for tomorrow. I can dance and sing in the wild abandon of inhibitions as I offer up praise to him for being the one that has never let me down. More importantly, I am never put in the position of having to figure it out on my own and make up for the lack of fulfilled promises with my effort. I can fall entirely into the faith that he said he would, and it shall be done.

Journal

How have you felt abandoned in your life?

How has God been there for you even when you maybe didn't see it?

Are you ready to let go of the past and draw near to God, who has always been near to you?

Action Steps

- Write down the moments when you felt the most struck by abandonment but then finish each sentence with but God was there.
- Read that out loud, and then imagine that moment, and God is right by your side, willing to carry your pain.

Dare

Whoever you have been holding back from for fear of them one day leaving, let go and leap. God will catch you!

Prayer

Father, I just ask right now that you come near me to feel your presence. Comfort me so that I can know you are here. Heal my heart entirely of the pain left after feeling cast off and set aside. Help me to have a deeper understanding of your word that says you never left me alone and prevent me from feeling this way again by helping me seek you out when I think others have left me behind. Thank you for being the constant that I have always wanted and needed, and thank you for never breaking your promises. I know that now I am free of all residue and behavioral issues that stemmed from feeling abandoned. I am Free to learn from you. Thank you, Jesus.

4

LONELINESS

"The most terrible poverty is loneliness and the feeling of being unloved."—Mother Theresa

Being lonely seems to be a pretty simple concept. Many people would put themselves in the category of having struggled with or are currently dealing with loneliness because they are not in a relationship or maybe don't have quality friendships that they can rely on. Some feel this deep longing to be in a meaningful relationship, and with that, there are always, every day, constant reminders that they are alone. As they watch people starting relationships and getting married, they can't help but think about their situation feeling so utterly left out. I can't imagine how hard it could be to trust God entirely for your spouse and not try to take matters into your own hands.

I applaud those who hold out for the one they know that God has brought into their path. Although they may struggle with feeling lonely at times, they are not willing to compromise. That is one area where I have an enormous amount of respect.

When my mother and father were finally done, God took the desire for him away from my mother, which meant she could move on with her life and no longer deal with him hurting her repeatedly. It was like an addiction that God helped her altogether remove. Since then, my mom has never dated another man. She has mentioned so many times that God satisfies her, and she is not in want, and I am so thankful for that. But I am even more grateful that she decided not to date because she couldn't be too careful with protecting my sister and me from another man as we were growing up. There were so many selfless acts, but this one, in my opinion, ranks at the top. She wasn't willing to compromise.

I could pretend that I related to this kind of loneliness, but in all honesty, I met my husband when I was 19, and I was married the month before my 21st birthday. I didn't have to go through this long period where I dealt with a strong desire for a companion without finding it. I am so blessed to have found this awesome man of God at such a young age.

But I am no stranger to loneliness. Mine was just of a different kind. If loneliness is an area where you struggle, you may have just rolled your eyes at the last paragraph. If I were you, I would have. I admittedly do not know the struggle of waiting and wanting for years to find a helpmate. But I want you to continue and try not to compare the battle. Let us focus on getting to the victory that God has for those that are lonely.

My loneliness was the kind where I would be in the middle of a crowded room, and I didn't know why I was there. I often wondered if anyone would care if I disappeared. I had this deep chasm in my heart that I was longing to fill with something, and every time I tried another option, I would end up feeling like a stranger around my friends. I was what some would call the runner. I would be sitting at a party with people that I thought I liked doing things I didn't know if I liked but wanted to try, and all of a sudden, this deep gaping hole would appear. It was like all of a sudden, I was this hollow, empty shell, and I could see right through myself. I would become aggressively introverted as the night progressed. I would be in my thoughts, and I would just stare at the people around me, feeling like they were strangers to me regardless of the relationships that were built. I felt surrounded yet alone.

I felt as though no one there could even begin to understand what I was feeling, so I never tried to talk about it, but it caused me to feel such devastating isolation, I didn't know what was wrong. I longed for a deeper connection. I longed for people that loved me and understood who I was. I wanted to have meaningful conversations, and when that didn't happen, I would just shut down.

After a certain amount of time, it would cause me to feel too anxious, and I would start to panic. It would always come to the point when I just had to leave. It didn't matter where I was or who I came with. I would get up quietly and make my escape leaving anyone behind because I had to be alone. It's like my surroundings had to match what I was feeling on the inside. I never knew why but at the beginning of the night, I would always insist that I drove because I always wanted to be in control, never being stuck or stranded anywhere when this feeling would hit me.

I had no idea what my heart was searching for, and I had no idea how to get it. I just found solace for the night and did all the explaining I had to do to my "friends" the next day.

This is the loneliness that is so concerning to me because it is so confusing and crippling. This is the loneliness you feel when your soul is longing for its counterpart. A counterpart that is not found in the opposite sex. You are longing for the one that completes you because it is he that created you. He is the only thing that can define you and sustain you because He fashioned you. That counterpart is God.

The people dealing with the loneliness that comes during the time frame of waiting for your spouse are in two categories: the weak or the strong. I don't mean that to be degrading. The "weak ones" will end up going through some not-so-good relationships because they have lowered their standards, hoping to make it easier. I was in that category, yes, even at my young age. Before I met my husband, let's just say I made some questionable decisions. I was weak and mainly because I wasn't connected to the source that gives the strong ones their power. I didn't understand it, and it would baffle me the faith that some had, but the bottom line is that they focused on their relationship with God, and because of that, they were made strong in the waiting process.

That is what I didn't realize was missing. I would find myself utterly alone because it's almost like God was calling to me. I would hear it like a whisper, and suddenly the desire to listen to that whisper would override my desire for all other things. When I heard it, my spirit recognized it. There I was doing God knows what, but my spirit man was in hiding because it didn't connect with any of that junk, and then God would speak, and suddenly, I was alone. I think that there was protection in those moments in hindsight. At the time, I just felt like I would never truly connect with anyone. I laugh thinking about it now, but I thought I was this deep soul meant to wander the earth alone. Finally, I realized that was silly, and I wanted to solve the problem.

I didn't want to feel like that anymore. Truth be told, if I didn't fill that gap in my life, then I would end up feeling lonely in any of the roles I had in the future. I could feel extreme loneliness within my marriage if I was expecting my spirit to connect with my husband's and at that moment feel complete. God is the only being that can make me feel whole. I would have ended up jeopardizing my marriage because I would have felt isolated all of a sudden, and in turn, it would have caused me to think that maybe I married the wrong person. Like the people looking for someone to complete them, my husband is not my completion. He is my companion, he compliments me perfectly, but he is not why I no longer feel alone.

I am a deep thinker, and my husband just isn't. There are so many times when I am trying to explain something I am thinking or feeling to him, and he is just not connecting because, to him, things are just simple. You always hear that the opposite attracts, and in that way, we are opposites. In marriage, you can be understood, or you can feel isolated if you don't feel understood. When you are deeply connected to God, you will always feel understood.

And when I was young, precisely what I needed at my core is to be understood. I decided to seek this God that kept speaking to me, this crazy magician that could make me alone in a crowded room. I decided to welcome him into those scary parts of me. During this time of seeking, I intentionally isolated myself. I knew God, but I hadn't indeed allowed him to penetrate the darker sides of me, I had let him play in the kiddie pool of my heart, but it was time for me to dive deep. I ignored the requests for my presence in all the places that I used to go. I forced myself to be alone because I realized I could no longer hide, and God was singling me out. I had to get and feel truly alone and then learn how to correct that feeling with the presence of God and nothing else.

This process was challenging, and there were many tears because the real me was being revealed. I realized the mistakes that I had made and the person I was becoming. I let myself get torn open so that God could get rid of the ugly and make things new. I had friends that told me I was betraying them and accused me of not caring. I even had a long-term boyfriend that I had to let go of finally, and his accusations were piercing, but I knew I was doing the right thing. I knew I was on the right path and with the right people when I no longer felt like I was alone with a group. God was fulfilling me so that I could add to others out of the overflow I was experiencing.

That is when I built the proper foundation with God. I got to a place of fully knowing he was with me. I knew I would never be alone again. If I were exiled or in a padded room (for a dramatic example), I would still be able to hear the whispers of my savior and feel his love radiate through me.

Whenever I feel like I am alone in something, I realize that I haven't connected well enough with my source. All I have to do is run to him and be alone with him and reestablish our connection and bond. You know how it is with the people that understand you and know you the best. It doesn't take long to pick up right where you left off.

If you're feeling alone, know that although God isn't a physical presence, he is the only one that can cause your spirit to feel understood, connected, and held. That the deep longing and loneliness you are feeling can be more than filled. I know that it seems impossible to cure that feeling with something you can't fully grasp but if you could just trust me on this one. You will no longer feel like the outcast in a room full of people who love you because you will feel love deep in your soul. That love will be all that you need. It will satisfy you. Then everything else is just a bonus.

Psalm 25:16 Turn to me and be gracious to me, For I am lonely and afflicted.

Have you ever been completely blown away by another person's honesty and admittance that they need you in their life? It is a truly humbling experience. They could have hurt you or done things you disagree with, but the second they admit they need you, things change. I have had in the past all intentions of completely severing a relationship. But things change when they acknowledge that they don't have it figured out and express that they need my help, I almost immediately go soft. How do you think God would feel? If at the core of him he longs to be with you, and you reach out to him. Do you think he will hesitate and say, "Well, I don't know, you upset me when you did that"? No way he is going to come to you and be gracious to you because he loves you, with a Love Unfailing and Unending.

Journal

Do you suffer from feeling alone?

What kind of relationship have you been longing for that you think will fill that gap in your life?

Have you ever considered God to be the answer?

Action Steps

- Reach out to a friend you can trust, let them know how you have been feeling, and make plans for some quality time. It is ok to let people know you need them.
- Also, go someplace where you are alone, a plus if you can be in nature and invite God into your loneliness. Ask him to come near and make his presence known and felt in your life.

Prayer

God, forgive me for not recognizing my soul's deep desire to be continuously connected to you. Forgive me for seeking out other things to fill the Gap that only you can. I am flattered to hear and know that you are Jealous of my attention and affection so I am coming to you and surrendering my heart. God clear me of the desires for the things that bring no fulfillment and hurt us both along the way. Infiltrate every space God and leave no room for the things of the world. I need your presence, your wholeness, and your peace to cure that deep yearning that I have felt. God rescue me from loneliness and be my constant companion. I need you now!

5

ENVY/JEALOUSY

Envy: A feeling of discontented or resentful longing aroused by someone else's possessions, qualities, or luck.

Jealous: Feeling or showing envy of someone or their achievements and advantages.

Jealousy is a form of hatred built on insecurity.

To be honest, I have always had and operated with a little bit of jealousy in my life. I thought it was natural and normal. I had never considered The Scripture that says Love is never Jealous and that I am supposed to Love all people. I am not perfect, and I fall short of that command in more ways than one, but I had dismissed jealousy in my life as something people just kind of deal with and ignore. I have never had the jealousy that has caused me to act out to discredit or injure my subject of envy. I would be lying if I said there weren't certain people in my past, and I hadn't at least had those thoughts.

I come from a home with a single mother, as I have previously mentioned. My mom was raising three children on her own. Although she did well financially, I was always still on the low end of the totem pole as far as the income bracket because we had only one household income. Also, because my mom had moved us to a pretty wealthy community to give us the best chance with our education, what I felt we lacked stood out even more than people with wealth. I always understood the decision she made to have us there, and I also understood our financial situation. I never became jealous enough of others that I put pressure on my mom to spend a bunch of money on things so that I could keep up with other kids. Honestly, I never would even tell my mom about things that I felt I was lacking because I knew in my heart that if I told her, she would find a way to make it happen. I didn't want her to do that for me. That doesn't mean that it wasn't hard. I was forever satisfied when we moved from the duplex we lived in for 14 years into a house. I finally felt like I was somewhat keeping up. I know my mom wanted to do it for herself, but I know for sure that she knew how happy I was.

I know all of this sounds like the basis of my jealousy was money, but honestly, it was more other things that I would find myself upset about. I was jealous of my friends that had two household incomes and not because of the financial situation that put them in but because that meant that they had a dad around. It also meant that they had a less stressed mom because not all of the weight fell on her shoulders.

I was so jealous of my friends whose parents were still married, and they got to see their dad every night. Oddly enough, I was even jealous of the kids whose parents were divorced, and custody was split. I had wished that my dad cared enough about me to fight for me. Instead, he just left. I wished my dad would pick me up for the weekend and take me to see movies, and invest in me. I wished my dad was just stable enough to have a place that I could visit, but that was just never the case.

When it came down to it, the lack that I had in the area of finances was never as big of a factor as the lack of a dad who cared. Now I am grown, and I have dealt quite a bit with the issues I had because of the lack of a father in my life, but I still get wildly envious when my other grown-up friends have a father involved in their lives. I learned I needed to fight it from going another layer deeper when I realized that meant my children would lack a grandfather. I have had to push back intense jealousy when friends of mine have had "inheritances" from their fathers or substantial chunks of money to help them pay for their wedding or their house, and it all boils down to the fact that I am jealous that their fathers cared enough about them to think long term.

Your jealousy or envy struggle could be with anything, and honestly, it could go deeper than you realize. From the outside looking in, it may have seemed as though I was mad that some people got lucky and had an excellent financial situation. In reality, I just wanted a dad. Don't justify your jealousy and be a victim, but at the same time, when it is something that goes deeper and at the root is something that is not your fault, then take the pressure off of yourself and deal with that root problem.

Sometimes we are jealous of people for things they are good at that we just couldn't cut it in. Like for instance, I am jealous of people with lovely singing voices. The fact is that singing is just not my gift. But you know what I can do, I can write. Instead of focusing on the one thing, you don't have as a skill set, focus on the things you do. Focus on your strengths and the things that set you apart, and stop focusing on every area you find yourself weak. When you look at someone else's life and see an area in which they are excelling, and perhaps you are maybe in your eyes lagging bust, remember they are looking at a different area of your life and thinking the same things. Just cheer them on and remember that God is not a respecter of persons. Believe that those same blessings are on their way for you.

Other people have nothing to do with who you are, where you are, and why you are there. The sooner you realize this, the sooner you can learn to accept yourself right where you are and be able to enjoy your life and its progression no matter what so & so's life looks like on Facebook or Instagram.

Ephesians 4:4 And I saw that all toil and all achievement spring from one person's envy of another. This too, is meaningless, chasing after the wind.

Gosh, I love this verse because It allows me to check myself. If I begin to toil and strive after things, then that is coming from a place of envy. I have looked at someone else and their success and decided that what I have is not enough. I know that God doesn't want me to be in a place of toil and rely entirely on self-effort, so I have always tried to monitor that, never really realizing why I would always end up back in that mode. When you are in that mode, you are chasing the wind, or in today's terms, you are spinning your wheels. YOU ARE WASTING YOUR TIME. Stay on track and focus on where God is taking you and less on where the people around you are going. Don't let jealousy cause you to begin to design a life that was never really meant for you.

Journal

What are the things that you find yourself looking at with green eyes of jealousy?

What is the one thing that when you see someone else with it, you are jealous, and it throws you into sweat and toil?

Does this Jealousy go deeper? And if So, try and identify what it is that you are longing for.

Action Steps

- Write a list of things that make you jealous.
- Write another list of things in your life that could make others jealous, give yourself some perspective.

Prayer

God, you are my satisfaction, and in you, I lack no good thing. You are the answer to all of my longing and desire. Strengthen me, God, and Be my blinders so that I can stay on the path that you are leading me down and not worry about where I am at in this race. Help me see what I have and help me no longer dwell on the things I don't. Give me patience for the things that are on the way but are not yet here, and help me learn to keep my words and faith lined up with your word, always in hopeful expectation. Give me revelations in this area, God, so that I may keep a fresh perspective and keep my focus on you.

Thank You, Jesus!

6

LUST

"There is no disease so destructive as lust." —Chanakya

Ok, Paige, you can just skip this topic because women don't deal with lust the way men do, right?
WRONG

Although this section is probably the most difficult for me to write, it can help many people. Lust is this thing that we shrug off as a battle that men have to deal with, and we women are just perfect in this area. It felt like if you are a woman dealing with lust, you should feel ashamed of yourself. It was almost as if just admitting it gives you the stigma that you are nasty, dirty, or filthy. However, if you are a man, admitting to dealing with lust is just being an average guy trying to deal with life's struggles.

In my everyday life, my husband and I mentor a lot of people. If people allow us to, we get down deep into their lives. We find for a lot of men; there is a struggle specifically in the area of pornography. But shockingly enough, I also found that when I admitted myself to having struggled in this area that all of a sudden, there were women that came out of the woodwork and said, "me too." Like me, they never admitted it because they thought they might be the only woman who struggled with it.

I took a massive risk of exposing one of my deepest darkest secrets, and what do you know, it ended up being helpful to other women I was mentoring in life. I helped unlock the shame they felt so that they could work on this issue. My husband knew about this part of my life because I have chosen the path of brutal honesty with him. At times, honesty was so uncomfortable. I felt like I was going to die, but he has always accepted me, heard me, and never judged me for who I had been.

So tell me if this sounds familiar to you "I am just a very sexual person." This was my "truth." I had no idea that it was my justification for why I had dealt with a lot of lust in my life. What I found out was that was just not true. That sexual person wasn't really who I was. I was a broken and hurting little girl that desperately needed help. All of this came to a head, and that statement was exposed for the lie that it was when I got married.

I had finally trusted God, and I did things his way. My husband and I kept our dating pure, and we waited to have sex until we were married. Entering our marriage this way was such a massive victory in my life. I was so thankful that my husband had a strong desire to do things this way with me regardless of the past.

This is awkward for me to say, but I am just real. Now that I was married and sex was a good thing, I was excited to unleash that "sexual person" in my marriage. To be honest, my husband and I have always had a good sex life, and I am incredibly thankful for that, but that is because I have been intentional. Pretty quickly, I realized that things weren't the same. The desire was there, and it wasn't about our lack of sexual chemistry, but I realized that I couldn't connect with my husband on the level that I desired.

My lustful ways of the past were all about the flesh, and I was longing for our connection to be more profound than that. I wasn't going to be satisfied with just sex. It was .hard to tell my husband that I was having trouble connecting with him because of my past and the enemy's lies, but I had to because I knew it wasn't what God wanted for me. I had chosen to do things God's way, so the enemy pulled the lustful rug out from under me, and all of a sudden, I was confused and sad, and I just wanted to shut down. I felt as though I had nothing to offer my husband, I realized that it wasn't ok to shut my brain off anymore.

I knew my husband, and I had made the right choice, so I wanted to fight. This was when I started opening up to him about who I used to be so that he could understand why I was struggling so much. I felt like I was being punished for all the things that I had done. We sought out some associate pastors in our church at the time, and I am so thankful we did. They spoke life into us, encouraged, and prayed for us. That gave me the strength I needed to fight and made me feel like maybe I wasn't the only one in the world to have struggled in this area.

I have found out that the thing you are trying to hide has more power over you the longer you keep it hidden. I didn't want to tell my husband what I had done, my addictions, and all my secret sins, but once I did, I was truly able to gain my Freedom over them because I could no longer hide in it. You think you are keeping your sin hidden from the world buy you are just allowing there to be this dark corner in your life that you can hide a part of yourself in. Expose it, shine a light on it, and you will no longer be able to run off to that place anymore. How awkward would it be if you had to participate in your secret sin with an audience of the people you love and respect?

It would be terrible, and as a matter of fact, you probably would choose not to. Further than that, I think you would decide you never wanted to do that again. It wouldn't be as big of a struggle anymore. That's how I have chosen to see it. I speak my truth so that there is no place to hide. I told my husband the things that tripped me up and the things that I would consider triggers. For me, that could be watching movies with sexual content or suggestion. I know the internet, and social media sites contain many triggers for a lot of people. I told him the things that would cause my mind to wander to that dark place. I also explained to him the patterns that had become a part of my life, the things that were the hardest to break.

I took this process seriously. This is a huge area of victory, where before, I had felt powerless and like I was never going to be able to shake it now. I barely remember what that plaguing feeling felt like. I no longer feed that lustful flesh. I starve it.

I have had to ask God to come into my marriage and guide me in my sexual relationship with my husband. I want our marriage to be all that God intended it to be without any of the perversions of this world.

There is so much more to this topic, but there is just one other area that I feel is so important. I came to the point where I felt like I would be doing so well, then out of nowhere, I would just give in to the lust, and I would be so mad at myself. I thought that maybe this was something that I would never be able to get past, mainly because it had been a part of my life since I could remember. So for one, if you mess up, don't beat yourself up. That is not going to help the situation whatsoever. You have to forgive yourself as God has forgiven you. But for me, I had to know, Where did this come from? When did this start? I asked God specifically, "why am I like this"?

It was something that had been a part of me for so long I

thought that it was just who I was and there was nothing to be done. Then hearing things like God doesn't make junk and doesn't make mistakes, I knew something had to have brought this on. I began to ask God for clarity and revelation in this area. It took A little time, but I started to have memories and recall things from my past. Something that I had blocked out of my mind, but vivid pictures began to appear and come to life once the door was open. I don't have all of the answers but let's just say some of those memories that had a bitterness to them had deep roots that directly connected to my lust.

Not only that, the time frame matched up. Without going into great detail, I was taught by a neighbor girl that I shouldn't have been taught. I was introduced to things that were the beginning of that path in my life at an age that breaks my heart. And at the same time,e so much peace came over me because I realized that it wasn't my fault. I wasn't born a sexual deviant like I had led myself to believe. I was a victim, and with that came even more release.

When it comes to cycles of sin, people that are naive to the struggle will always point at your choices. They will tell you that it is all about the choices that you are making and not giving room in your life for those triggers to appear. I found these things helpful, but only after I discovered the root of the issue. There is far more to stopping such an addiction than just starving the flesh. Knowing that this wasn't my fault was huge. For me to see that I wasn't, the issue changed everything. When people don't understand why they reach for their sin, they have trouble stopping even when they want to refrain more than anything.

Romans 7:19

For I do not do the good, I want to do, but the evil I do not want to do—this I keep on doing.

In this scripture, you see Paul is struggling with a cycle of sin, and his answer to overcoming that sin wasn't just I am going to start making better choices. The power of God had to overcome what he was dealing with.

Won't you allow God to take you through a healing process? It may be scary and awkward to even admit this stuff to yourself, but God will lead the way if you want to be free.

Galatians 5:16 So I say, walk by the spirit, and you will not gratify the desires of the flesh.

It is not like your flesh will not have desires, but when you choose to walk with Christ, he empowers you, and with that empowerment, you will have little time, energy, and desire to satisfy any of the things that your flesh may long for. That was the part that was most helpful to me. I just realized that I couldn't do it on my own. I didn't have the strength, and I needed God. And still, so many people struggle with this, thinking that God is just going to take the desire and addiction away. He can. I am not saying that God can't but what he wants is for you to take the time to invite him into your day and walk with him. When he is a part of your life in that real and intimate way, he will be the guiding force and strength in your life.

Journal

Have you ever been plagued by lustful thoughts?

Have those thoughts driven you into lustful actions? If so, do you want to be free, and how have you sought this freedom in the past?

Take it a little deeper

Where do you think all of this began for you? Do you need to forgive yourself and or someone else?

Action Steps

- Bring it to the light, and let go of the lust. As long as something remains in the dark, it can plague you, talk to a trusted confidante and let them know of your struggle.

Prayer

Father, I am your child plagued and afflicted by a sinful nature that I no longer want to be a part of. I need you to show me who you say I am and wipe me clean of who the world and the enemy have tried to convince me that I am. Jesus purifies me in your love and makes me whole in you. I give over my heart and all of my desires to you, and today I ask for you to meet me here and be in control. Give me your heart, give me your wants and help me to walk accordingly to your spirit and not my flesh. I also erase every plaguing memory and every destructive thought that has led me into lustful patterns. In the name of Jesus, I break those chains off of my life, and I am no longer a slave to that sinful nature. I forgive myself and anyone who initiated that behavior in my life. Jesus in you today, I am made new.

Praise Your Name!

APPROVAL ADDICTION

The greatest prison people live in is the fear of what people think.

"God created us to please him, which sets us free from the need to please people."—Joyce Meyer

A person who struggles with an approval addiction must have the approval of others in their life. Without that approval, they lack, and it causes them to strive. I think at some point in our lives. We have all dealt with this in some manner. For most people, you have suffered from this during the dark ages of your life called high school or in that one relationship that you felt you had the most to lose. Typically this is a season in life where you are trying to fit in or not trying to lose someone that probably shouldn't be apart of your life in the first place.

It's a natural stage to go through while learning who you are and who you want to be. When we are young, we are navigating through so much, and we have so much going on in and around us that life is just more manageable if you are well-liked. Honestly, you may not be liked by everyone, but if you have a couple of people who seek to understand you, you will be ok.

I remember going through this season. I remember some of the things I did to belong, make people laugh, and try to win them over. But I also remember when the switch began to happen. When I started to see pretty clearly what was real and what was fake, the moment that I realized the majority of the people that I had kept myself busy trying to please were themselves also putting on a show, I gave up. I decided no matter what, I was going to be unapologetically me. I was going to speak my truth and not care what anyone thought.

Then there was the learning curve. I realized maybe it wasn't always necessary to say exactly what was on my mind and that in the attempt to be myself, I was reckless with the feelings of others, so obviously, that had to be corrected.

I was in a place in my life where I didn't care what others thought, and I didn't care how that made them feel.

The one fact that strengthened me with every day was that yeah, I had something to prove, but that was to myself and my God. Everyone else could love me or hate me, and it wouldn't make a difference in the end.

Approval addiction comes in and begins to run your life when you realize that you do have something to prove. Only you get confused when you start to believe that the world is the audience you are trying to convince. Instead of living life performing for a deserving audience of one, you begin to live your life performing for people who aren't worthy of your efforts. In that process, you lose sight of the art, the beauty, and the self-expression in it all. Instead, you focus on what will get a response, what will generate the oo's, the ahh's, and the applause, all of it in desperate striving to maybe just maybe one day receive a standing ovation.

You become the person who overdramatizes everything so you can pique their interest and keep their attention. You are the pretty little horse on the carousel going around and around to entertain and delight others to remain well-liked.

None of this is technically wrong. You aren't hurting anyone when doing this. You become a person that people gravitate to because no matter who they are, you will be the person to tickle their ear with some fascinating story. If you don't know what they are interested in, you stroke their ego with compliments. You aren't lying as much as sometimes just stretching the truth a little bit to make everything a little bit more appealing, just a little bit more sensational. The problem is not others and the effects on them. The problem is how this type of behavior affects you.

Exactly how much of yourself are you letting appear? Deep down underneath it all, there is a vulnerable person in there underneath the facade? That is the real you that never gets showcased and therefore never connects with anyone or anything. Are you ever actually able to connect when your number one plan is to make sure that everyone around you approves? How long will you be able to keep up with all of this before you slip up and make a mistake or exhaust yourself to the point where you begin to search for what can fill you.

When you never want to let anyone down, and you always want to be well-liked, everyone gets a piece of you—even the people who have no business inquiring for your attention. When you have a problem with someone walking away with a less than stellar opinion of you, it becomes easier for you to lower your standards. You may not even have a good impression of that person, but heaven forbid they walk away with the same thoughts about you. That's going to make it hard for you to tell someone with a vulgar mouth that you don't appreciate that type of language. It will be tricky to shut down flirtatious advances from someone that is not your spouse, or if you're single, someone that you know you don't need to be getting involved with.

It's not the need for approval that is the problem but more what that need often leads to is the bending and breaking of your moral compass to remain liked.

Your approval addiction will drive you to be the person that fulfills the desires that other people have because, in turn, they will praise you for that. So my question is, where does God stand in all of this?

When is the last time you took a moment to ask the only audience member that even matters what his review is on the life you are living? I don't think when I was so focused on what other people thought of me. I even took the time to consider what God thought of me. When I dressed for others, I didn't consider his opinion, and if so, would he have approved? I can 100% remember too many moments where I shattered my moral compass because what would that person think if I stood my ground at this moment. Would they stop liking me if I did not participate, and what would they then go and tell others? You don't just want remarkable personal testimonies to how much other people like you, but you want their raving reviews. You want them to spread the news that you're the bee's knees.

God is so unimpressed by all of this, mainly because you're ruining your chances at not only a deeper connection with him but with others.

So here is your moment. Who are you, and who are you NOT. Honestly, you might want to start with the NOT list. Start stripping away what you are not at first can help you focus on what's left. You will have so much more to offer people when what you are offering is real and rawly authentic.

Back in high school, I should have made a not list that said:

- You are not a rebel.
- You are not a rulebreaker.
- You are not rich.
- You are not disrespectful.
- You are not a "sexual person."
- You are not the toughest chick around.
- You are not a player.
- And on and on and on.

Leading right into

- You are the girl who has to work "daddy doesn't pay for everything."
- You are hurt that you don't have a dad.
- You are silly, goofy, funny, and wild.
- You are the girl who wants to fall in love.
- You are the girl who hates disappointing her mother.
- You are Loyal
- You are the coolest if you let them get to know you.

Make your list, and please think about you right now as you are. I go back to that example because it is the most relevant for me. Use who you are right now at this moment. You don't need anyone's approval, not even your own. Get brutally honest with yourself and force the digging on this.

If you do, you will uncover a well of YOU. A new life that is springing up from inside of you and wanting to burst out. The energy inside of you is not meant to entertain other people or get them to like you. This life that will burst forth is the you that will bring a refreshing to those around you. It will stir them inside to want to be more real and a desire to be better.

Sometimes, the freshness will come in the form of you having to walk away or state that you don't appreciate something that is happening or being said. Although someone may walk away feeling that they may no longer care for you, their character wants to rise to be better on the inside. Darling, don't seek others' approval because honestly, you will never have it, seek the approval of God. Then seek the woman's acceptance in the mirror. She is your harshest critic, and if you can win her over, you have won the real war.

Galatians 1:10: For am I now seeking the approval of man, or of God? Or am I trying to please man? If I were still trying to please man, I would not be a servant of Christ.

I just love the word of God. When people, myself included, are confused, I genuinely3 think it is because there is a lack of the word present in their life. Everything I said is summed up in such a simple manner. If you are focused on pleasing people, then you cannot also be serving Christ. If I have rubbed you the wrong way, the word just lays the hammer down plain and simple. We were not as Christians created or meant to live our life to please anyone but God. And in a moment, life just got a whole lot more straightforward.

Journal

Who are the people whose approval you seek the most?

Have you ever tried giving them the real you?

Do you think God is pleased with the person you have been
lately?

Action Steps

Make a list detailing who you are not (but maybe you have tried to be).

Make a list detailing who you are when you are not trying to please anyone.

Prayer

God, I come to you right now in no performance, but with my heart, I want to connect to you, the one who created me. You have made me authentic and wonderful, and I know you want to see those qualities shine. Forgive me for faking it for this long, and forgive me for not seeking out your thoughts in all of this. You are the one that I most want to please, and I have at times lost sight of that. God reminds me of your presence daily in my life and stirs me on the inside to give others nothing but the real pieces of me. Strengthen me in your approval and help me to shine through in this world. Strengthen my resolve to always stand for who I am and who I am supposed to be no matter who is watching and what they think. I speak right now, Jesus, that I am released of the opinions and man's approval through you. I am free just to be me. In your name and your power, Jesus!

8

FAVORITISM

Favoritism; the practice of giving unfair preferential treatment to one person or group at the expense of another.

I can't even believe I am adding this one because seriously, I am so convicted just even thinking about it myself. I'm over here like, is this one even needed here? All the while in my mind, I am thinking (I know I do this on occasion.....ok all the time, but so does everyone else, right?).

Even more honesty for you, I am just now realizing that this is an issue in my life because when I was just flowing with the holy spirit and writing out all the potential roots that women are struggling with, this one just flowed out through the keys and showed up on the screen and I am all like WHAT?????

That's so rude...

What kind of grown woman would behave in such a way?

Ok, Ok, but here is the thing, these people that I "favor" that you are steady trying to convict me about just understand me more. Those other people just don't get me...

WOW!

Ok, that sounded bad because it came out sounding kind of like it is all about me.

Let me start over.

Hi, I am Paige, And I struggle with favoritism.

The whole goal of this life as a Christian is to become more and more like Christ. Luckily he didn't play favorites. He didn't live his life picking and choosing the people he would spend time with based on how much they had in common or how much they understood him. On so many occasions, his disciples would shock Jesus with how little they seemed to understand his teachings. They would even question his methods. Had he been "choosey" like some of us, there are for sure a few Disciples he may have started to ignore, maybe even woke up early to head off to the next town without.

He knew people to their core, knew their faults, and even knew the things they would do against him, and still, he chose to give them a chance to be a part of his life, his ministry. He was the epitome of patience, preferring to see people with the end goal in mind.

That's also extremely fortunate for the people he healed. He didn't ask first if they were from the same town as him or check out their garments and decide that he couldn't heal them because they just didn't have the style he was looking for. When I put that in this context, it sounds ridiculous but have you ever stopped to analyze some of the initial thoughts you have that either drive you towards or away from someone. Typically when you see someone with a similar style or even one you admire, you gravitate to them. But if they dress in a way that you never would, you tend to keep your distance. We judge people based on what we can gather about them from afar.

Sometimes we allow people just a little further into our

bubbles to get a better feel or because situations and circumstances forced that. Like maybe the usher sat you down in a church next to someone you have seen every week, but you have never said hello or even introduced yourself to because they don't "seem like" someone you would connect with. There you are, though, sitting next to them in the church seats. You are so close that your arms have touched multiple times. In those situations, we are forced to talk to someone we wouldn't typically, but what is so silly is that still, we don't even give them a chance.

We give them the best surface-level small talk that we think we can muster up, but we don't just dive in.

Maybe this isn't you, and perhaps I am just talking to myself, and if that's the case, that is fine. You can skip ahead to the next chapter. Some people will open up the door to another with no pretense, and I respect that very much. That just isn't me or hasn't been met in the past. I have been hurt enough in my life where I was forced to put up walls, but unfortunately, I left them up. I found myself opening up a pretty wide door for visitors to come in, but eventually, they would need to leave. I only let my walls down for a select few.

I was an open book for the people who made a friendship easy, the people that were similar to me.

For those of you who I don't understand, our personalities don't line up, and I just don't get why you do the things you do the way you do them; WELL.......

In the past, for those people, the chances were that we just weren't going to end up getting that close. I wasn't going to put forth more effort than necessary to understand you or to be understood. I would be friendly, and we could get along, but we would never really be friends.

I operated like this for longer than I would care to admit, and honestly, in some situations, I can still find myself falling into playing favorites because it is just easier that way.

I would be lying to you, friend, if I changed on my own accord and, out of the goodness inside me, strived to be better in this area. What happened was I got to a point in my life where I was tired of being misunderstood, and I was tired of dealing with people that did not seek to understand me and my methods and the deep down why behind them. I was so drained, and I thought to myself, I am pretty awesome, and I am worth getting to know, I may be different, and in a lot of ways, I can be challenging, but everything I give to the people that allow me to is worth all of it.

Then I had this beautiful God moment where he slapped me across the face with a severe reality check. He began to show me people that were in my life that I have ignored. People that look up to me or have sought me out, and because they were so far outside of my box, I would just shoo them along. It's not that I was ever malicious, but I was 100% being selfish, and even thinking of it brings me to tears. I was doing to them what others had done to me. I pictured specific people, and God began to show me deeper into their hearts. It was like all of a sudden. I saw these women as the radiant creatures God had created that offered so much that I couldn't even bring to the table. I no longer saw them as the difficult ones or the projects. When I would think of them and the things about them in the past that would frustrate me, it was like I finally understood where they were coming from.

God gave me an eye transplant, giving me his view of others, and I am so unbelievably grateful. I began to choose to see people a layer deeper and hope that people would see me in the same way. Because of this, I have developed a deeper connection to a few women that I just would have never really gotten to know. Because of this connection, I have been able to bless them, but at the same time, I have been able to learn from them. In your life, as you begin to mature and God's love inside you grows, you have these profound moments where you feel like you understand "Humanity" and what it means to play a role within it. In the moments where I chose to open up my time, my life, my heart to women that were so completely different than me, I realized that they aren't that different. That inside of all of us, these beautiful intricacies were designed to add value to others and bring color to the world that no one else can provide. We all long to be understood for what makes us beautifully unique.

I know this to be true about myself. I do know for a fact that when someone has tried too hard to connect with every part of me and prove how similar we were in efforts to deepen our friendship, I felt threatened as if my individuality was being robbed. I enjoy having things in common with someone, but I appreciate it when someone takes an interest in what makes me different from them.

I am now focused on bridging the gap between myself and people who seem to have nothing in common with me because if it's real and fundamentally different, then I am excited to learn some things that I didn't know.

I am sick of playing favorites and limiting myself and who I can become. I don't want to put my social life in a box, but instead, I want to be that person that can be comfortable sitting at tables with people that others wouldn't expect me to sit with. Suppose I am criticized for this. Well, then I have become more like Christ, and just as an additional reminder, isn't that the goal?

Matthew 9:10-13 While Jesus was having dinner at Matthew's house, many tax collectors and sinners came and ate with him and his disciples. When the Pharisees saw this, they asked his disciples, "Why does your teacher eat with tax collectors and sinners?"

Jesus knew that it was the people that didn't have him that needed him. I know that I am called to spread the truth of Christ and connect people to his great love and his never-ending grace, but I have also begun to take on a philosophy that has helped me no longer play favorites. I believe that if someone allows me into their life, it will only get better. But if I spend all of my time sitting with the people I already know, I am limiting how many lives I can enhance by being a good person and taking an interest in them.

You don't have to have a personality like mine to add value to the lives of others. People need you and those parts of you that are the opposite of me.

James 2:1

My dear brothers and sisters,[a] how can you claim to have faith in our glorious Lord Jesus Christ if you favor some people over others?

If you claim to be a woman of faith, then you must treat God's children with equal love and regard. I would encourage you to read on in James 2 to hear from God how he feels about playing favorites. I remind myself that I definitely wouldn't want God to begin playing favorites, which checks me.

Journal

In what ways have you struggled with favoritism in your life?

Have you been a victim of favoritism?

How do you plan to begin celebrating and enjoying the differences of others?

Action Steps

- Take the time to go to coffee with someone you haven't "clicked with" in your church or at your job and just try to learn something about them.

Prayer

Jesus, thank you so much for not picking and choosing the people you lived, loved, and died for. Thank you for your grace that has chosen me regardless of my faults and calls me worthy of such a fantastic gift. I want to do my very best not to let you down. I want to be like you to connect with people who need hope, desperate to be seen, and crying to be heard. Give me your eyes so that I can see them, God, Give me your ears so that I can listen to them, Give me your patience to try and understand them and give me your heart to love them like they deserve to be loved. I will no longer be a person that plays Favorites, but you empower me to show the ones who need it the most supernatural favor from a well that only you can fill. Use me, God, to bridge Gaps and break barriers in Your name Jesus!

9

LYING

Lying: statements used intentionally for deception.

The truth doesn't cost you anything, but a lie could cost you everything.

With Every single chapter of this book that I write, I realize that God is just using an incredibly imperfect woman to share with you all how flawed does not have to mean broken. I am incredibly humbled by this material. I have learned a lot, and I have grown more than I thought I would, so I can even write any of this. I am sitting here just gushing with thankfulness that God has brought me so far and that I can so freely admit to all of my flaws because God is making something extraordinary out of all of my mistakes.

That doesn't mean that it doesn't sadden me to admit that I was a liar at one point in my life. The only reason that it still strikes a chord in me is that I know that lying hurts people. That simple fact hurts me because I know that there is one person that I have lied to the most, and that would be my mom—the woman who was simultaneously laying down her life for me to have everything that I needed. I chose to be with her, a completely different person than I was with the rest of the world.

The truth is, the person I said I was; was the person I wanted to be. I just felt like I couldn't be that person. I didn't think anyone else would like her, and she was stronger than me. She made better choices than me and was much more of an independent thinker. I showed my mom the side of me that was true, but the lie was the person I was hiding.

I also give myself a lot of grace because I was a teenager at the time, and I was dealing with raging hormones and the lack of a father. I also had some pretty crappy experiences, but those are weeds that I don't want to get into here. The bottom line is that I lied all the time. I had to lie to cover up other lies that were all a part of an even bigger and worse lie. Looking back, I realize that the lies began to catching that I wish didn't happen, something that never should have happened. I began to lie to cover up the fact that I had been taken advantage of. I lied to cover up, feeling like an absolute fool for believing the one that lied to me. I lied, and I covered up the fact that I was hurting. I lied to cover up that I felt like I had lost the one thing that would have allowed me to be that person I wanted to be.

I could have told my mom the truth. That I was a good girl, with good intentions that had let myself be groomed for eight months by my best friend's older brother. That eight months to a 14-year-old was a lifetime, so if he had been trying so hard for so long, then he must have cared. I could have told her that I never meant to do what I had done and although I let it happen, I wasn't ready, and I truly had no idea what it meant. I could have told her that he took my innocence when I was at a sleepover with my best friend. I couldn't tell anyone I even liked him because if I did, then there would be no way that we would ever actually get to spend time together. The problem is that because I withheld that information, then my mom couldn't protect me. I had no one point out to me that I should be thinking about what his intentions may be.

I could have told her that he talked me into staying for the whole weekend, but on night number 2, after the deed was done, he went to hang out with his friends and other girls his age. I could have told her that I spent the night crying in the arms of his younger brother. The only reason he knew is that he had bragged to him about what he had done. I could have told her the truth the younger brother told me, which hurt so bad I felt like I couldn't breathe. I wasn't the first, and that the next night he was with another girl he was also dating. This younger brother wanted me to know the truth so that I wouldn't let him continue to hurt me, and he told me the truth without fear of consequences. That was such a brave choice that I didn't think that I could make.

I can imagine that she would have been upset, that she would have been hurt, that I decided. But I can also imagine that she would have chosen to be there with me and help me get through the intense amount of pain that I was going through. But when I got caught instead, I lied, which meant I had to pretend that I was ok. More importantly, I lied because I had already decided never to let it happen again, and I wanted to be able to pretend it hadn't happened at all. But that is where it all began, lies to cover up lies.

I was no longer that little girl with good intentions. I was a broken young woman that vowed never to let anyone hurt her like that ever again. So here I was, living this double life. I was for my mother, pretending to be the girl she thought I was, and I wished I was. All while on the other end, I was living like the shattered person that I had become. Lies have a compound effect on your life. And It gets to a point where you don't even know how to stop it.

The only fear that remains in speaking my truth on this matter is that there is still so much that my mom might not know. I don't want to cause her any pain or make her feel bad for not knowing the things I was dealing with at this point so far beyond those days. Although I tried to blame her for "not knowing me," it was never her fault. It was always mine because I told her I was okay. You cannot expect people to read your mind.

I finally got to a place where I began to live my life how I felt like I was always supposed to. I began to live for God and leave all of the junk in the past. I couldn't believe how natural lying had become, so it took some time to get a handle on it. I had lied so much for so long that when I didn't need to lie, I would still find myself lying about such little things.

I would be having a conversation, and maybe the person would be talking about this vacation they took, and I would ask where and they would tell me, and I would say, oh yeah, I have been there. And it would shock me because I was lying, and I had no idea why.

Lying was a part of my sinful nature, and I had to suffocate it for it to die off. I legitimately would be able to fill a lie coming up, and I would sometimes have to not say anything at all to not lie. Once I got to a place where I was no longer an active "liar," which felt good, I would be presented with lies from my past, and that was not fun at all. I had to choose to own my lies in multiple situations to feel like I could move on from them. Now I am not talking about every single little lie I told about the vacations I took. I am talking more in terms of the lies I told that affected other people.

I remember one lie specifically that I had told for so long ago over and over again that I had begun to believe it myself. This is an example of a lie that I was very ashamed of because it was so stupid. My grandpa came to stay with me while my mom was out of town, which never happened. During that time frame, I managed to hit the garage at our house with my car. The garage still worked, but it was a very noticeable dent that stayed with us for years. I told her that my grandpa was the one that hit the garage. That wasn't even to cover me for some deeper reason, like I was drinking. I wasn't. As a human being, I made an error, and instead of owning up to it, I blamed my grandfather, and I am genuinely mortified for that part. He was the best man on the entire planet, so yeah, that's terrible.

I can't remember when or why I finally just fessed up. I think it may have been after my mom finally got new garage doors, and once I was no longer under her roof, there could be no consequences... I thought she might get mad, but it had been so long, and my sister just laughed at me, but they did tell me how rude I was for blaming it on gramps. That was it. It was over. I mean, it still gets brought up during let's roast Paige hour, but honestly, I deserve it. People who lie to cover up lies are avoiding a truth that will cause far less damage than they imagine.

I also told my mom about a dent in my car and how an ex-boyfriend of mine had been the one who inflicted it. I lied because I didn't want her to know that I was dating someone abusive. At that time, the abuse had only been verbal, and I didn't want to tell her about this incident because it was the first time he became physical, and it would be the last. At least, that is what He told me.

So I didn't just lie to protect myself. A lot of times, I also lied to protect others.

Every line that I ended up telling the truth about relieved more and more of my guilt until finally, I was completely free of it all. Free from every lie that I know of and free from the liar himself.

The enemy no longer had this deep and dark secret to hold over me. His number one tool was no longer plaguing my life or my past.

If this sounds all too familiar and you maybe have been a liar too, I know it sucks to admit but let me tell you that you can also be FREE. No lie is worth the inner turmoil that it inflicts. We believe the enemy when he convinces us that lying will make it all go away, but the truth is that it gives him permission to dwell on the inside and eat away at us when we lie. He is the father of lies, and when we participate in it, we invite him into our lives. No matter what the truth is, when you Lie, it makes it 1,000 times worse. Maybe not right away, and perhaps it seems to help the circumstance at the time, but what it does inside of you will never be worth the temporary relief.

Luke 16:10 One who is faithful in a very little is also faithful in much, and one who is dishonest in a very little is also dishonest in much.

This scripture spoke volumes to me because, in such a simple way, it tells you that lying is a slippery slope. Although it may start small, it begins to grow and become a part of your life. People do not think that the little lies matter, but they help lower your standard, making it easier to tell the lies you feel you would never tell.

Let's release all lies and their infection of our character today.

Journal

Have you ever found yourself in a web of lies, or maybe are you caught in one right now?

Where did all of it begin?

If you are ready to be done with all of the lies, how do you plan to start? What is the first truth that you can tell?

Action Steps

- Confess a lie.
- Tell a truth.
- You are already convicted, so I am sure you know which one.

Prayer

God of truth, I need you right now in my brokenness. I speak an untangling right now of all of the lies that I have allowed to enter my life. I ask for forgiveness for the lies I have spewed from my mouth. I will no longer be caught up in lies, but I will wrap myself in the truth of the living word of God. The liar that has tried taking over my life is no longer welcome, and I will no longer live in the false reality his lies have built. God take me from this point on and guide me in what's real and what is right, and I pray for quick future conviction if I ever flirt with that line again. From this point on, I will be truthful through the power of the holy spirit living in me. Amen.

10

GOSSIP

A gossip is a person who habitually reveals personal or sensational facts about others.

Surround yourself with people who talk about visions and ideas, not other people.

I have personally been learning so much about the words that I speak. I have been focusing on this area and watching my mouth. In this process, I realize that so much of our conversations are filled with unintentional gossip.

There is so much about social media and how people share information these days that almost deem it ok. People either overshare things that I would consider personal, or they hint at them, whether intentional or unintentional. Then, people share on social media or hint to become public knowledge and therefore the topic of your next conversation with someone who also knows the person who posted the juicy information. The problem is that most of those conversations can tend to be very critical even though it starts as two people just sharing their thoughts on a matter that another person brought to life.

If you are anything like me, you have caught yourself in the middle of a conversation going in a very negative direction, and for whatever reason, you know better, but you don't stop it. To make matters worse, if I am frank, I have had conversations like this that I knew were wrong, and I knew I had gone too far, but I didn't care because maybe I did strongly disapprove of the topic's choices. I have tried my best to be the person that won't say anything out loud, that I am not willing to speak directly to the person's face, but I have failed at that many times. It is something I work way harder at today. It crosses the line into gossip when you know you either know you wouldn't say what you are saying to the person you are talking about or when you know that you wouldn't want them to know that you are passing along this information.

The hardest part of society today is information is like currency, and some people feel above others when they carry information that the other person doesn't have. It's like it releases endorphins in some people to be able to pass on sensational details. The problem is this is only fueled by the reaction they get to said shocking information. It makes it so difficult on both ends not to give or receive the info.

There aren't too many people I know that have mastered the art of avoiding gossip. I know that my grandpa was the type of person that would discourage gossip and slander. Even if that person had hurt him, he would refuse to entertain that type of conversation. It wasn't worth it to him. To most of us, to talk about people and the "sensational" things going on in their lives seems worth it because of the rush of "KNOWING." It's exciting, whether it be good news or drama, it's like we oo and ahh over what is going on in other people's lives. It provides a wonderful distraction from what is going on in our lives.

When we hear of bad news, it spreads so quickly. Even though it is sad when someone has passed or been in some kind of accident, people still love to share the news. Today sharing information that is not our own is prevalent. It's a massive part of how we live. There can be an article posted that shares information, and although it doesn't pertain to you or isn't your information to share, you do so because you know it may be of some interest to people you know. I am not calling this gossip. I am just saying that this type of information sharing that we are so used to makes it harder and harder to operate with discretion in any area.

As for me, I have no desire to be like everyone else. I don't want to knowingly sin just because it is so prevalent in society or because it will be challenging to conquer this issue. I believe that anything fleshly that I find challenging to overcome is a great invitation for the holy spirit to show off in my life. To invite him in to help me guide my tongue and even my ears in conversations that I need not be a part of.

For me, it is simple. Divorce is pretty common in society today, but that doesn't make it ok for me. I don't judge anyone else and the situations that have led them to that place. That is not for me to do. I just know that just because others do something doesn't make it ok for me. Just because things can be hard doesn't mean I should just give in. That's how I feel about gossip. I always want to carry the holy spirit, and if I am continually dabbling in conversations that offend, then the spirit will not be able to remain.

Maybe you will find that you have allowed a lot of gossip in your life if you start paying attention. Perhaps you will find that people always tend to bring the information to you or even come to you to get the information. I have been both in the past.

I have had to learn to be careful with what I choose to listen to and what I choose to tell people. I work with people and mentor them, so I hear what is going on in their lives. It is vital that I not share personal information with others. The only time I share is when I have permission to communicate certain things to my mentor to gain a higher perspective. I am disciplined in this area because I have zero desire to betray someone's trust. Outside of my mentor/mentee relationships, I have been loosely lipped with information and justify giving and receiving information because it is just the way of the world. We live in the information era. One of the most convicting things for me was thinking about how damaging it could be and how much trust I would lose if I were loose-lipped with the information I had been given in confidence within a mentor/ mentee relationship. Once trust is lost, it can be tough to regain, and I don't want to have to go through that just because I wasn't mindful of my tongue. What is worse is that once you lose their trust in some people, it is gone forever, and the conversation that led to that could never be worth such long-term damage.

What if I choose to dialogue about the information made public, and I do so in a critical manner. I think we can sometimes justify ourselves because I wasn't the one who shared the info but now that it is out, I will say what I think about it. But the person on the other end could be sitting there thinking, " do they talk about me and my issues the same way"? I don't want anyone even to begin that type of thought pattern.

As far as Gossip goes, there are so many different ways to look at it and think about it. There are more scenarios than I could think of. So I just read the word, and I see what it says on the matter. I invite the Holy spirit in to guide me, to tame my tongue, purify my lips and bring that same purity down deep to my heart where all of my intentions live. I can say that even though there are some people that I have my struggles with that I would never want them to hurt or be hurting. Words that don't bring life are precisely the opposite. It may seem severe to say that because you would never kill someone, but you do when you speak words to them or about them that don't give life. Maybe not literally or even immediately, but you bring death to their situation. I know that is not what anyone intends.

I can fully admit at this moment right now that this is an area that I still have a lot of work to do, and I am excited about that. Even though it may be frustrating to some, and in some cases, I may be considered "no fun," but I want to be that person that will remove myself from conversations that turn to gossip. I want to be the person who can speak words of life over anyone brought up in a conversation in a critical manner.

I welcome being annoying to others as long as I am pleasing God by following his commands.

Try it this week. Pay attention to your conversations. Be sure that you aren't the one to bring up anyone and their situations. When someone else does bring something like this up, say something positive about the person and if it continues, then walk away. You will be willing to do this as long as you are not more concerned about man's opinion. I dare you to choose words of life this week and see how it makes you feel.

I guarantee you will feel more of the positive and "happy vibes" that you've been missing.

This quote has challenged me to my core in this area.

"Great minds discuss ideas; average minds discuss events; small minds discuss people." —Eleanor Roosevelt.

I remember the first time I heard it, and I was offended because I was mortified to be finding out that I had a small mind the majority of the time. I knew for a fact that God had called me to be excellent in every area of my life. I wanted to be significant even in the types of conversations I have. Tonight I am speaking in front of my church about IDEAS I have for our ministry, and consistently I talk to people I mentor about the ideas that I have for their future and my own. I have chosen to upgrade my speaking to prove to God that he has made a great mind, and I am not going to let it go to waste by always chattering about people and events.

Journal

Has this topic of gossip convicted you?

In what area do you feel most convicted to watch your conversations?

Action Steps

- Do your best to have only positive conversations today. If a discussion goes in a negative direction, then find a way to turn it around.

Prayer

God, your word says that no man can tame the tongue so that I will need your help for by your power, and through the guidance of the holy spirit, I know that I can be someone who brings life through my mouth. I can choose to talk of only the things that are good, lovely, and pure. Convict me, father, when my conversations stray from what you would find pleasing because that is the goal, to please you in every way. I want to be the person that challenges those around me, not makes everyone comfortable in their negativity. If that makes me unpopular, so be it. I want to bring glory to your kingdom, father. Be with me, father, be with my mouth. Thank you, Jesus.

11

CONTROL

Control: the power to influence or direct people's behavior or the course of events.

I will never forget the moment when I realized I was a bit of a control freak. I wish it had been a shocking self-discovery, where I could then quietly reflect and decide to change my ways. Instead, it came in the form of my best friends ganging up on me at a sleepover. They had the best of intentions, they did, but they lacked tact in their approach.

They said, "Paige, your so bossy," and gave me an ultimatum. I was funny and wild, and they loved that, but my strong natural skills in leadership spillover, and because of that, I would limit everyone else around me.

It wasn't that I didn't like who they were and what they brought to the table, but I thought that if we all followed my plans and ideas that we would all have so much more fun. I honestly had no idea that I had just been controlling my friends.

Although that moment hurt, I can say that it benefited me in the long run. I was more aware of those things going forward. In ways, I would taper down to have better relationships with those around me. I continued and just learned how to be more subtle with my control or tactful in my approach.

The truth remained in my mind that I was a natural-born leader, and I would not apologize for that. Honestly, I didn't work well with others who felt the same way because there could only be one leader in every environment, and it was always going to be me. These other strong personalities would either have to fold, or our friendship wouldn't work out.

Control, though, definitely wasn't one of my major issues until I was pursuing my relationship with God. It may have been to the people around me, but it benefited me, so I didn't care. But as I began to develop my relationship with God, I had the realization that actually, there was very little I was in control of, if I was honest with myself.

Then it became a problem when I got married. I had this deep desire to be led by God and let the man I felt he put in my life Lead me. I didn't have that father figure in my household, and instead of rebelling against that home-style, I wanted to embrace it. The problem is that I was only willing to embrace it if he could just lead the way that I thought he should.

Sadly sometimes, that is the way I was with God as well. I desired to work in my life and accomplish what he had meant for me to achieve, but I wanted to do it my way. Along as I was going in the direction, I knew that he wanted me to go, then what did it matter how I got there? What was confusing to me was that God wasn't willing to help me in my disobedience.

It was hard for God to bless me even though I was pursuing things that were good because it was all in my control and in my doing, which just meant there was very little room for him to do his part. Trust me. You want God to do his part. Everything was more complicated than it needed to be, and there was so much more force to it. Of course, this just led to me getting frustrated and then taking it out on people around me because I thought I had everything under control, so if things weren't going the way that I thought they should, then surely it was someone else's fault.

I thought I was " all over it in every area of my life," so I didn't understand why it was causing so much stress and anxiety. For example, I handled the finances because I didn't trust my husband to do as good a job as possible. I tracked everything and even did crazy things to overcompensate for some mistakes I had made in the past. I would make my husband text me every single time that he spent money so that I could track it. Honestly, we were doing great for our age. We weren't hurting financially, so there is no reason why I needed to be so detailed I was just a control freak.

In turn, It just so happened that finances were something that I thought about all of the time. I was always stressed and always worried, even when there was nothing to worry about. When I felt convicted about my control, this was one of the first areas where God told me that I needed release. I needed to trust my husband to take care of this, but I also needed to trust that God would handle it as well.

When I gave that up, it was hard at first, but now even if I wanted to check our bank account, I couldn't because I don't know the passwords anymore. I forgot them a long time ago. Nor do I care what each of our accounts looks like, and that to me is so much freedom. I know some of you out there like, well, if I did that, then bills just would not get paid. Well, maybe that would be a wake-up call for your spouse. Some of you are single, so please keep being responsible with your finances. I am saying that I made this shift in my life out of obedience to what I felt God was telling me to do. That doesn't necessarily mean that I am giving you the same advice. This is just one area where I was able to feel so free because I released control, and God knew that I needed that.

On a day-to-day basis in business, I was unknowingly using many control tactics that just aren't fair. Because of my lack of trust and faith in God and what he said he was going to do, I would try to control the people around me to reach the goals that I had for my life. I was having people make decisions that were in my best interest and maybe not theirs, and that is very hard to admit. I quickly realized the error in all of this. I was not just controlling but extremely manipulative. But there was one that would never comply and that I was never going to manipulate, and that was God. God was not going to be controlled, and he most definitely wasn't going to be mocked. He made it abundantly clear to me that this was not the way to get what I wanted.

There were things that I needed to change about myself, and that would be a prerequisite to seeing growth in my personal life in my business. I knew this, and I was just trying to avoid that hard work of improving myself. I wanted to force others to make up for where I was lacking, and that just wasn't going to fly. That may operate well in some environments, but that control tactic didn't line up with my heart and what I wanted for the people that God had placed in my life.

I began to release that control and that taskmaster off of my life one step at a time.

Then I got pregnant with our daughter, our first child. That is when I realized that there is nothing in this world that I am in control of, and here there was this little 6lb baby girl that was proof of that. When that fact hit me like a ton of bricks, I chose to embrace it rather than denying it.

Some people have children and then become much more rigid and controlling. I let it all go finally, and I became much more laid back. I guess I just realized that there is no way that I could have on my own produced something that beautiful and perfect. Had I tried to do things in my way, she wouldn't have made it. So If letting go and trusting God can produce such a remarkable result, then I may want to begin doing this more often.

That is the thing that ultimately I am trying to say. Being a person who controls things may make you feel robust right now, but what actual result does it produce? What does it create in your marriage? In the lives of your children? In your friendships or work relationships? But most importantly, what does being in control produce in your relationship with your heavenly father?

What father wants to be told by his spoiled little daughter that she knows the best way to handle this? Even worse to be told to back off, and even though I want you to let me handle this, I also expect you to show up when I think it is time that I start seeing some results. Wow, I cannot even imagine my daughter saying that to me. Unfortunately, that is how God is feeling with some of you right now. It is ok, I have been there, and you can release all of that instantly.

Proverbs 19:21: Many are the plans in the mind of a man, but it is the purpose of the Lord that will stand.

I feel like every scripture that I provide is so simple, but seriously, let us not overcomplicate everything. We get so caught up in making all these plans and trying to execute everything with perfect precision, but right here in the word, it plainly states that the purpose of the Lord will stand. So with or without your grand plans, God will get his goal accomplished...

In the words of Elsa, "Let It Go!"

Journal

Do you feel heavy, like you are carrying everything in your life on your shoulders?

What areas do you need to release control so that you can remove the weight?

Action Steps

- Choose one area where you can let go of your reins of control. Maybe it can be left alone, or perhaps you know that you can delegate, but you haven't.
- DO IT, JUST ONE THING!
- FEEL THAT FREEDOM!

Prayer

God, would you forgive me for being a control freak. Forgive me for hijacking the plan that you have for my life and trying to make it my own. I know that controlling things will not produce the result that I want, so I ask for your help. Could you help me to release the control I have operated in with the people around me? And I release full control to you because I trust that You will do the job much better than I will. Help me to know going forward the things that I just need to let go of. I wish to be free to let your will be done in my life, Jesus.

12

FEAR

Fear: an unpleasant feeling triggered by the perception of danger, real or imagined.

"Fear has a large shadow, but he is small."—Ruth Gender

I am sure that everyone has heard the acronym for fear, false evidence appearing real. Fear is your response to evidence that something coming will be either dangerous or harmful in some way. There are some situations in which fear just needs to be checked and moved on from. Then there are some situations in life where fear is natural because a coming situation is dangerous. Maybe you or someone you know is about to have a dangerous surgery but could save their life. There is a certain amount of natural fear in that.

What about the person who has had extremely high standards placed on their life, and so far, in everything they have done, they have excelled. But because of that pressure, they live in constant fear that they will mess everything up. They are tormented by the thought that the next thing they do could be the first thing they fail at. That is a fear for people like that because they would find out that they are not perfect. That may seem simple to you, but some live in the dread of that. This type of fear is self-imposed but be brought on by the pressure from those people/parents who think they are just being supportive and helping the person reach their full potential. In all reality, the pressure they are placing will likely create a more significant issue long term. It can be a selfless fear that, in some way, you are going to let down those that love you the most.

Then, the fear awakens in a person's soul when they innocently experienced something they shouldn't have. It was so overwhelming and out of nowhere, something they never worried about or never thought would happen to them. Then they come away from the situation with a fear that it will happen again or that anything could happen if that could happen. They almost begin to take on Murphy's law because of the awful and random act that altered their worldview.

This is fear that you cannot blame someone for.

As Christians, we sometimes blanket sweep so many things when life is much more complicated than that. That doesn't mean that God cannot handle it all in one swoop. I believe that if he said all matters of fear flee Now, they would. When we operate in the power of Jesus, we too can blanket sweep healing and faith over that fear. But sometimes, we also need to understand that fear can be the fruit of other deeper root issues. Sometimes fear is the symptom of the sickness of abandonment, rejection, abuse, and so much more.

When we blanket sweep fear as something people just need to get over, we take away the validity, and when someone is told that what they are dealing with doesn't matter or doesn't exist, we are telling them inadvertently that they are crazy. When we bunch together all fear like it is just something silly, we discourage people from seeking help. We tell them it isn't real. It doesn't matter, that would never happen, that won't happen again, you're seeing things, you're overreacting. What's worse than being afraid? Being afraid and feeling crazy for it.

When A child is told not to be afraid of the dark and the things they are seeing, they are told that they are crazy and their mind is playing tricks on them. It would be helpful to remind them that no matter what, Jesus is with them, and there is no reason to be afraid because Jesus has overcome all darkness and things that lurk there. When we don't see something the way someone else does, we tell them that it's not so, instead of just handing them the weapons they need to fight the things they fear.

We tell people that to fear is weak. That makes it seem as though since they have the fear they have already lost, and they might as well give up. People are made to think that those who accomplish things in this life have no fear, which is just not true. Even Jesus was beginning to get apprehensive about that danger he was facing. He asked for God's will to be done, but he also said that if God could take the cup from him, that would be good too. He faced a REAL enemy and a REAL threat. How silly would it have been for his disciples to have said, " Jesus, chill." He would have said, you don't know what I know, and you haven't see what I have seen. God instead gave him the strength to overcome the fear that he felt.

What I want to say to you is that because you have fear doesn't make you a failure as a Christian. Maybe it makes us around you a failure because we have failed to help you in identifying the root. You are not broken and faithless without hope of ever being a victor or an overcomer.

Now let's give it to God.

I am telling you right now that you are not crazy. That everything you Fear had a root, but God desires to uproot all of that and equip you to face it with his power.

Isaiah 35:4 says to those with fearful hearts, "Be strong, do not fear; your God will come, he will come with a vengeance; with divine retribution, he will come to save you."

This scripture doesn't indicate that God is ashamed of you for being weak and afraid. It also doesn't diminish fear as if it doesn't exist. It acknowledges it and addresses how God intends to help you overcome it. His power is what reduces it. In the face of his authority, it is not real. God doesn't think you're crazy, or else he wouldn't promise here to be the one to save you.

Journal

You can, and you will overcome this but first, tell me, why are you afraid? Do not tell me you don't know, come on, you will have to do better than that. Dig down deep inside and tell me when did or does this fear arise in you? And why?

Does it bring you back to a moment in your life where something terrible happened, so you choose to give in to fear because that's better than feeling the pain of the past?

Whatever your answer is, I want you to write it down.

What is fear holding you back from?

Action Steps

- Choose something to do that will show boldness in the face of your fear. Let me put it this way.
- DO ONE THING TODAY THAT SCARES YOU!!!!

Prayer

God, right now, I give this fear to you and speak that Fear has no place in my life. It will not control me and will no longer hold me back. I am free from the painful memories that the enemy uses to cultivate fear. I am free from the restraints that the enemy has tried to place on my life. I am free from the situations of my past. I am open to pursue the life that God has called me to. Every day in everything I do, God is with me, and when God is with me, whom, what, why should I ever let fear have any place? I walk with The great I am, the one who was there initially, and he will be there in the end. I carried the resurrection power inside of me that conquered death itself. What could have more power? No devil in hell can come against that power, and I walk in that authority now and forever!

SPEAK THIS EVERYDAY IF YOU NEED TO!

13

DEPRESSION

Depression: feeling down or unhappy in response to grief, discouragement, or disappointment: if ongoing may indicate depression.

"There are times when explanations, no matter how reasonable, just don't see, help."—Fred Rodgers

These days this word is so common that there is no need to give you a definition. I don't think there is anyone who has not been directly affected by depression. Whether you have dealt with it or someone close to you has it, it has hit home in most people's lives. There is so much negativity in this world today that there is no shortage of reasons for someone to be sad but then add to that all the personal tragedies that happen in people's lives.

Nowadays, it's so common to meet someone and think they have it all together "there is no way this person has ever been through anything," you say to yourself. Only to hear someone's story, and you wonder how they have even made it this far. Unfortunately, this happens all of the time, and because of that, what is expected is that someone just moves on and deals with it. And some people can do that. But then again, Darling some can't, and that is ok.

Some may not be able to process such pain like others, and that pain can lead them down a dark path where depression becomes a part of their life.

Or maybe you are going down that deep dark path, and you have so much guilt because nothing that bad has ever happened to you. You just can't seem to get happy.

I will be honest with all of you and say that Yes, I have dealt with seasons in my life of depression, but I did not let it run my life. I refused to let the negative things that hurt me steal my life by dwelling on them. I never wanted to be a victim. Now before you skip this part because you are sick of being told that, slow down.

Having the mentality that I would not be a victim in many seasons was why I dealt with depression. Instead of saying, hey, this happened to me, and it hurt, and I need help. I chose to "not let it win" or "not give it light," so I kept it all in. That festering was what drove me into sadness. Then what made it even worse was I began to feel like I missed my chance to be the victim, so then I thought my time for healing had passed. Any time I brought up people acting as a victim in a judgmental manner, it was because deep down inside, I was jealous of the attention they were getting for the areas they were hurting.

I would get so mad that others were catering to people who had been through far less than me. Because honestly, I needed to be cared for, but I wasn't willing to admit it. I considered those people weak without realizing that they have to exercise a great deal of strength to be that vulnerable to expose that they are hurting.

So, although my process of dealing with depression was very internal and God had to do the work all on his own. He did it, and he will work for you too. But I think he may have used other people to help him with my healing if I would have let anyone know just how much I was struggling.

Thank you for continuing to read. What I am saying to you is that it is ok to be hurting and to admit that. It is okay to open up to people that you know have your best interest in mind. It is ok to be weak and human and be open about your pain.

When a child is sick, they tell their parents so that it can be decided what the child needs to help get them better. Sometimes that is rest, sometimes, they need medicine, and sometimes they need to see a doctor. But If the child doesn't let the parent know, then the parent cannot do their job in making sure that the child gets well. That is what makes having a small child who cannot yet speak so nerve-wracking because that child cannot say what is wrong and what they feel, so you have no idea how to make it better. You have to trust your instincts to guide you and pray that you are doing what is right.

Trust me; although you may not believe this, there are people in your life that feel like this with you right now. They know that you are hurting, but you just won't talk to them, so they have no idea what to do or how to help. If you are blessed, you have people in your life that will let the holy spirit guide them in steps to helping you get better. But not everyone has that. So help your friends and your family out. Talk to them. They want to know what is going on with you. Yes, they already know you're sad! NO, you are not that good at hiding it. I know this is a scary place for you, but it is scary to the people who love you.

There are answers for you, and there is healing for you, and the most challenging part of it all is saying that you are hurting.

Don't be like me, don't keep it all in. I am one of the "lucky ones," even though I don't believe in luck. I pressed into God enough for him to take over, but it scares me to think what would have happened had I not had that relationship established. What would have happened to me if I would have kept all of my darkness hidden inside and I never pursued Jesus. I would have either lived a life of quiet desperation or have not been able to live, and that is unnerving.

Yes, God can replace your sorrow with Joy instantly, but he can also use the people in your life to help you along the way. He can equip them to be the community that you need when you feel so alone. To be the light for you when everything just seems so dark. He can even place people in your life that will bring clarity to all of your cloudiness if you are willing to be open to that.

If you are that one person that doesn't feel like you have anyone close to you, reach out to someone in your church. Ask God to show you who, and he will. If you don't have a church try finding one in your area and connecting with people. It may be a crazy concept, but you will find good people if you get into a good church. You don't have to know someone for years to open up to them. Let God build a bridge and create bonds for you. You don't have to follow the rules of engagement that the world goes by. God will knit someone's heart to yours. He will make someone's mission your happiness. I know this sounds like an impossibility, and to the world, it can be, but it is what we like to call a miracle, and God is in the miracle-working business.

Worst case scenario, reach out to me. There is contact information in the Bio Section of my book, and the least I can do is help you find resources. I would even sometimes suggest traditional counseling to those who don't at this time in their life feel comfortable pursuing "church people" because I get it.

You may have initially thought that this is just who you are, and this is how your life will be. You may have thought that you would be sad like this forever. You may feel like your happiness is broken. I am here to tell you that God can and will guide you closer to him and his love, and he will fix you.

I remember a season of my life where he was doing major surgery on me when I was depressed and lonely and didn't know if I wanted to continue. I was lying on my bed listening to music with headphones on and crying quietly. God can use anything at any moment when he is trying to reach you. I asked him how he could ever make this right, how I would get past the pain, and then a song came on that rocked me. I listened to it over and over and imagined God was speaking the words to me. It was Fix You by Coldplay. Look at the lyrics if you feel like you could use a little bit of that right now. The only part of that song that I must dispute is when he says, " I will try to fix you," I know God doesn't just try anything. He does.

There is nothing that he cannot do. That darkness does not belong in you, that is not how he created you, and that is not how he wants you to live your life. He has planned good things for you. He has prepared joy for you. He has designed for you happiness and a life of purpose.

Suppose I can offer you just one other tip. Outside of finding someone you can confide in, you also need to be sure that you are not isolating yourself. Reach out to friends and make some plans, do this in good faith that you will be getting better. When we feel sad, our instinct is to isolate, but that will never help us feel better. I believe that fellowship with people that love you can bring immense healing to your soul, and laughter is some of the absolute best medicine. Who makes you laugh? Get around that person!!!

Romans 15:13 May the God of hope fill you with all joy and peace as you trust in him so that you may overflow with hope by the power of the Holy Spirit.

It is all by the power of his spirit that you step out of such sadness. We try to do so much on our own and figure it out on our own. We just need to realize that without God, we are a terrible mess. But sis, with him you can be so happy!

Journal

Are you ready to be happy?

Do you feel like you know what makes you so sad?

Do you feel like a last-ditch effort you can try, and I mean try to let God Help?

What is a change you can make this week to show God you trust in him to fill you with joy?

Action Steps

- Think about a time you were really happy. Recreate that moment! Get together with the people you were with or do the thing that you were doing.

Dare

- Pick your favorite praise and worship song and put it on repeat! Belt it out until you begin to feel joy fill your heart!

Prayer

Father, I give my heart over to you right now. At this moment, I feel sad that I no longer have the strength to remove. I need your help, reach deep down into my soul, and uproot every bit of sadness and pain that remains in me. God replace all of that with your goodness and let JOY burst out of me at this moment. I trust in your promise that goodness will follow me all of the days of my life. From this moment on, the Joy of the Lord will be my strength, and I will walk in that daily. In Jesus' name.

14

EMPTINESSS

Emptiness: the state of containing nothing.

"It is funny how the absence of something is the heaviest to carry."—Anyshree Joshi

As if one topic was more problematic than the other, when you are talking about humans and the conditions we face, each has its challenges. One thing that is vital to recognize with each of these roots is the circumstances that planted them in you. That is what can cause one issue to be above another in your life. For me, emptiness is one of the hardest. It is not because it was the hardest to get over but more because it was the hardest ailment to give up. I felt in all transparency that I deserved to feel that way.

Ok, friends, if you have gotten this far, I feel like we have gotten pretty close, and I can just go ahead and take the plunge into the deep. If you are still reading either, you pity me, or it is safe to say that you have issues too, so no judge zone, right?

You hear so many bits and pieces of my story throughout this book. I write this with courage because I want to heal others by exposing the scars of my past. I also think about my mom and hope that she doesn't ever read some of these heavier things and feel responsible. There is an enemy roaming and seeking to devour, and he has wanted to ruin my life since I was young. Maybe he knew if I could make it this far, then one day, I would be sitting here in a coffee shop writing this healing book to others.

There are the things that I can blame him for, and then there are the things that I take responsibility for. In certain seasons of my life, I was hurting, which caused me to make terrible decisions that flowed out of that place. When I was 17 years old, some consequences had caught up with behaving like I was invincible. I could have had so many other things happen to me because sex wasn't the only thing that I was allowing myself to be reckless with. But I had been far too careless, and I ended up pregnant by an off-and-on-again boyfriend.

I was in a place that I never expected to be, but I don't know why other than just being so naive. I cannot tell you how many conversations I had up until that point where I swore up and down that if I ever ended up in that situation, I would just buck up and own the consequences of my actions. But then it happened to me, and I could no longer sit in that judgment-seat complete lack of perspective. In those moments of being so afraid, so humiliated, so ashamed, I made one of the worst decisions I have ever and will ever make. I chose to end an innocent life through abortion.

I will spare you all of the details, but I can honestly say that I just had no idea of the situation's gravity. I didn't understand anything about this child and the stages of a fetus. I cannot entirely blame the clinic because I chose to take responsibility but what I will say is that they had me convinced that this was no big deal and it wasn't even a baby yet, and so on. They didn't tell me that the baby inside of me had a heartbeat. I think had that information been exposed. It would have become so real. Instead, in my shock of just not believing I was in that situation, my surprise was coddled, and they took the "problem" out of my hands.

Just like that, it was done. You know the statement, "you don't know what you have until it's gone," it was almost like in an instant I fully understood what that meant. I went into the whole thing reluctantly but also thankful for an escape. I walked out knowing that I made a mistake. I know for some that would turn into wild and exploding emotions, but for me, it was like all of the life inside of me was gone, and there was nothing left.

This is the season of my life that I call the walking dead. I went about my life like nothing had happened, but I had nothing left to offer. I didn't tell anyone, and I went about doing the things I had to do, like going to school the next day, but I began to keep to myself.

This went on for a while, and I had no idea how to remedy the problem. I didn't know how you could put life back in me and why I would even deserve that. In my mind, I was the worst type of person. I had always thought I knew what kind of person I was. I thought I had presets, and all of that proved wrong. I was empty and a stranger to myself. Only a few people in my life knew and had no idea how much it bothered me. We just continued living, but I felt nothing. I thought about it every single day, and I can say, for the most part, I still do.

Darling, I have no idea what has brought emptiness into your life. I don't know if me telling that story has struck a chord, and maybe you have been there. Or perhaps something else has happened to you, and you almost wish you felt pain because it would be better than feeling nothing. I hear you, and to be honest, that is the route that you may have to take.

I cannot tell you exactly how it should happen for you but what I do know is that God will fill the most barren places in your life. Even if you feel like you don't deserve it, I know that I didn't. I had thrown a gift of his in an industrial waste bin and walked away. How could I ever be worthy of him, let alone another gift from him? I would sit in services that would bring up abortion, and they would say you can be forgiven, but I was in no place to receive anything. I believed I could be forgiven, but I didn't think that I should be.

Then I heard a testimony from a woman who had made the same decision. In that testimony, she talked about how she knows God has forgiven her, but then she said something that changed me. She said that she knew that her baby was in heaven and that she would meet him or her one day. And then, like a bolt of lightning hitting me for the first time, I felt. For the first time, someone helped me to validate the life that I gave up. That it wasn't nothing, it was a child, and that child deserved a chance. The pain hit my abdomen and then ripped through my entire body, and I allowed it to. That pain was my grief for a child I lost. I welcomed the pain because for so long, there was just nothing and nothing is what I felt I had deserved.

Have you ever thanked God for the pain? At that moment, I did. I thanked him for letting me feel again, for allowing me to mourn for my baby. I asked his forgiveness, and then it came with such amazing grace. That not only was I forgiven but one day, when we are all with the lord, I will see my angel baby in heaven.

But that was just my story of emptiness. Maybe yours looks radically different.

Maybe you are dealing with infertility, and month after

month, when you start your cycle, you face the overwhelming feeling that you are empty once again. You long for your womb to be filled, and in your waiting, that emptiness has become your identity. Maybe even reading what I wrote above makes you resent me a little. That is fair. When I made that choice, I had this overwhelming feeling of guilt because, for three years, my sister tried to get pregnant and was unsuccessful. I remember knowing that she was trying and just watching time go on and on. I would remind myself of how I gave up the one thing that she wanted so badly. One time we sat in the car, and we prayed together, and at that moment, I felt so selfish. So I get it. Hearing that what you desire other people are receiving and not appreciating sucks. What I get is that I cannot imagine the struggle you are going through. I just believe that God wants to fill your life with your heart's desires and what it looks like right now is not the final answer. Can you dare to believe in that? No matter how empty you feel in the moment!

Maybe a loved one was taken from you too soon, and you have gone numb to protect yourself. I understand. Empty just seems so much easier, but nothing fruitful can flow from that place. And more importantly, no matter what has happened, even if you feel like it is your fault, God does not want you to live like that. The whole point of being here is to be fruitful to be able to love his people. What kind of love can you offer anyone from a place of emptiness? He wants to bring the fullness of his glory into your life.

God can, will, and wants to fill you to overflowing with His Love, His power, His forgiveness, His Healing, His spirit. He wants you to feel in order for you to be felt. So it is up to you. Do you want to remain this way, or do you want to be filled?

God can make you whole, and he is the only thing that can. There is one warning that I feel is appropriate to mention. That as humans, we are natural seekers. If you are empty, you will naturally gravitate towards things that you think will make you whole. I went into this season first before I allowed God to come in and take over. I was trying to feel something, contain something, and everything I tried was either a fleeting high or a shovel that dug me to a deeper place of emptiness. Maybe you even seek to feel pain, so you cut because once again, that is better than feeling nothing at all. As well as I do, you know that nothing good can come from that cycle. So why not let God do it and don't try to do it on your own. Give it to him.

More importantly, welcome him into your life. If you think you have done that but still feel emptiness invite him deeper, surrender more because it would be impossible for you to feel empty when he comes. There is nothing better to fill you than the presence of God. When he fills, you nothing is lacking and nothing you will want for.

Psalm 16:11 You make known to me the path of life; in your presence, there is fullness of joy; at your right hand are pleasures forevermore.

With the presence of God, you will not just be filled with Joy, but you will begin to enjoy life once more.

Journal

If you have gotten to a place of emptiness in your life either now or in the past, what do you feel caused this?

Have you tried to get fulfillment on your own, and if so, how has that worked?

Are you ready to let God bring fullness?

Action Steps

- Make a list of good things that fill your life. Then thank God for all of those things and ask him to add more.
- God will bring you to the place where "your cup runneth over."

Prayer

Jesus, I ask in this moment of complete emptiness that you come like a flood of crashing waves. Take me as I am now, empty, numb, and lifeless, and bring me back to life. You carry the power of resurrection and to revive a barren womb. I require your wonder-working power right now at this moment. I cannot live another day without your all-consuming presence in my life. Come, God, I give myself fully and completely over to you right now, fill me with your life and heal me of my past that has robbed me of life right now, Jesus. Thank you for being the God that fulfills every void. You have restored my life, and I dedicate it to you, God.

15

GUILT/SHAME

Guilt: the fact of having committed a specified or implied offense or crime.

Shame: a painful feeling of humiliation or distress caused by the consciousness of wrong or foolish behavior.

Grace means that all of our mistakes now serve a purpose instead of serving guilt and shame.

From reading the previous chapter, I wondered why I went into a season of guilt and shame. Although I consider all of the things that I went through to have been a part of the healing process, I look back now. The moment after receiving forgiveness, I had so much confusion as to why I began to feel this way.

I knew that God had forgiven me, and I was at peace regarding that dynamic, but when it came to the way I felt when I was around people, there was so much guilt and shame. I had always felt like I had a calling on my life, but all of this negativity felt like a threat to that future. I thought that I was this person forever ruined that had no right to ever speak into the lives of others. I was ashamed of my past and the countless foolish decisions I had made. I thought that maybe someone would find out who I used to be, and they would expose me. Then everyone would know how much of a fraud I was.

It's so silly when I look back at it now because there isn't one person that hasn't made mistakes apart from Jesus. Even when reading the bible, there were characters that I looked up to for what they accomplished for God. So because their story stood out to me, I dug into their story further. Then I was also like, wow, these people are messed up. Like really God? Was there not anyone else available for you to use? Even Moses, who led God's people to Freedom, had been a murderer in his past. This type of truth brought so much freedom to me. Throughout the word of God, you find people with ugly pasts and yet and still when they were just obedient to the call of God, and they overcame their past to accomplish so much for the kingdom.

My sweet friend, there was a moment in my life when I would never have shared what I have so far shared with you. The reason was that I had more fear of the opinion of man than of God. I have since then adjusted that, and I can say that I am more afraid of not doing what God has asked me to do than I am of what others may think of my painful past. You can get to that place too. Your guilt and your shame have no place when you operate in the presence and spirit of God. He has cast your sin away and says it matters no more. He also wants to lift off the dirt placed on you by others. Your only sin from a crime committed against you is if you chose to let it ruin your life. All you need is to give it to him.

Once you have taken care of that with God, in His presence,

and through reading and studying his word, once you indeed have received the good news that he has washed you clean, you must quickly tackle the way you feel about any of that being exposed to man. I know full and well that there will be people who will say negative things about me and my choices. If I plan to uncover the truth of healing and forgiveness by telling my testimony, there will most definitely be people who will want to slander me. There will be people who would, regardless of how far in my past something was or how God has already forgotten it, would like to see me stand trial for those sins. What is even worse is that they want to be the judge, the jury, and the executioner.

Forgetting their sins, people want to point out the flaws in you. The number one fact to remember in situations like this is that your war is not with flesh and blood but spiritual warfare. Know that anyone that could ever hear a piece of your past and hold it against you is being used by the enemy or just desperately trying to mask their secret sin. The one that would see you ruined for your mistakes. You can let go of all of that right now by realizing that not one single opinion from another person matters when you know what God has said on the topic. There is nothing that you have done that is worth threatening your future in Christ.

I remember my past boyfriend once I told him my secret he had promised to protect that information. Then when we would get into arguments, he would say to me that I was damaged goods. He often reminded me that I was stuck with him regardless of how volatile our relationship was or how many mistakes he made because no one else would want someone as broken as me. He made me believe for a time that he was the only one that would accept me, even though he would also verbally abuse me for those things that I trusted him with.

He was used as a tool to distort the way I saw myself. With every word, he intended to lower my standards and weaken me so that I would stay put. What the enemy couldn't control was what happened when my spirit recognized the truth in the word of God. I would hear things that would speak directly to my soul, something like you are worth far more than rubies, you are fearfully and wonderfully made, God has plans for you, plans to give you hope and a future. My spirit would lift because it knew the truth, so I allowed those words to pierce me.

I left the relationship I thought I would be in the rest of my life. I left it in the same place I left all of the lies in the past. To get past guilt and shame, I had to remove myself from people who would throw it at me.

I chose a relationship with God where I knew that he would never put my past mistakes in my face no matter what. God didn't want to hurt me in that way. In fact, he said he had forgotten all of it, and he wanted me to as well.

You are not broken, dirty, or damaged goods. You have simply just allowed lies to infiltrate you. The only thing that needs fixing is your input, what you are letting go in. It might be negative words coming from others or negative things you say to yourself either way. You need to get good at detecting what you allow and don't allow in.

One of the best ways to combat the things that the enemy will try to tell you is to know what God says about you.

Here are a few scriptures that you need to speak over yourself.

Scripture Affirmations

Psalm 139:14: "I praise you because I am fearfully and wonderfully made."

1 Peter 3:3-4: "Don't be concerned about the outward beauty of fancy hairstyles, expensive jewelry, or beautiful clothes. You should clothe yourselves instead with the beauty that comes from within, the unfading beauty of a gentle and quiet spirit, which is so precious to God."

Song of Songs 4:7: "You are altogether beautiful, my darling, beautiful in every way."

Psalm 46:5: "God is within her. She will not fall."

Proverbs 31:25: "She is clothed with strength and dignity and she laughs without fear of the future."

Psalm 34:5: Those who look to him are radiant, and their faces shall never be ashamed.

Going forward, when lies begin to attack you, all you need to do is cross-reference them with these scriptures. When you are rooted in the truth of what God says about you and how he feels about you, then guilt and shame begin to fade. You will realize that you are a precious Child, loved by a good father, and his name will protect yours on this earth. So often, when I think about the Father and his love for his children, I am reminded of the love I have for my children. Although I must make sure they are trained up, sometimes they must be disciplined, which does not diminish who they are in my eyes. If someone tried to remind my children of their past mistakes continually, I would be pretty quick to correct them and remind them how awesome they are. Your father in heaven has the very same regard for you. He doesn't want you or anyone for that matter, tearing you down for the things in your past. So I stand tall, knowing no matter what bully may ever come against me from my past, my Dad has something to say about it, so I will run to him. He will tell me who I am and what I mean to him, and then nothing matters as long as I have the approval of my father.

Don't try to argue with the bully in others or the bully that has tried to reside in you. Let's uproot that bully now and take out guilt and shame once and for all.

Here is an exercise that I also want you to try. I know it can help you. It has helped me. Pull up youtube and listen to how he loves us by David Crowder band. Close your eyes and truly allow the words to sink into your soul. Darling, he is Jealous for you. He wants you and your affection more than anything. When you truly know that and believe that, all becomes right in the world, and all of that guilt and shame is no longer even a thought.

Journal

Write down as many good things about yourself as you can think of. Let's drown out the bad with the good! This may seem weird, but I have had to do this at different points in my life.

Don't start small!

Write 20 good things, and if you get the momentum, keep going:

1. _____

2._____

3. _____

4. _____

5. _____

6. _____

7. _____

8. _____

9. _____

10. _____

11. _____

12. _____

13. _____

14. _____

15. _____

16. _____

17. _____

18. _____

19. _____

20. _____

Action Steps

- Write out your guilt and shame list, and then get rid of it! (throw it in the trash, rip it to shreds, or burn it if you want to get crazy, just do so carefully).
- Speak out the affirmations in this chapter!

Prayer

God, it is humbling for me to hear that you, the father of the world, is Jealous for me and my affections. To know that you would as a good shepherd leave the 99 to find me the 1, the one who is feeling pretty lost and pretty worthless to you right now. But then over the hill, you appear, and you are looking for me. I am in awe of you, God. I am in awe of your love for me, and I am honored to love you in return. I know that your love fills me so much that guilt and shame will no longer have any place. The words that you speak to me fill me. God just continues the rescue mission in my life. Help me erase my past's bitter memories that allow me to receive the guilt and shame. I speak that any words that are not of you are foreign to me, and I will immediately deny their passage to my heart. I will receive only your words, I will accept only your love, and I, with your help God, and through your strength, I cast off every bit of guilt and shame right now and speak freely through and through.

16

TRUST ISSUES

Distrust: the feeling that someone or something cannot be relied on.

Trust takes years to build, a second to break and a lifetime to repair.

This one is too easy to talk about. It is one that I feel like is the most widely spread, though. It is not as significantly looked down upon. Honestly, I feel like people now wear distrust as a badge of honor. It speaks of their past and the strength they have to be where they are still standing. But it ignores the simple fact that you are caring around pain and unforgiveness and, even worse, the bitter memory of what caused you to lose your trust.

I remember being that person. I felt it made me look tough to bring up in conversation, especially with people I was just allowing in and getting to know. I would explain how I didn't trust anyone. It's like saying, "you are privileged because I don't allow people in." Some people let a ton of people in and still claim this. Some people with trust issues still have a pretty open border. As for me, that was not the case. I had a tiny inner circle, and most of my circle was my guy friends. Honestly, I told myself that it was about girls and their drama, but it was because my guy friends very rarely dug into my past and my pain. They just were, and they let me be. I could trust people that I didn't have to give much of myself. Girls were scary because they wanted to be let into your heart. Girls want to feel like they know you by finding out intimate things about you, and if I opened that door, the chances of being hurt were high. I had done that, and I had been burned, Bad. I mean, I could tell you the story of 8th grade and freshman year that could easily be made into a teeny-bopper movie. I went through some of the craziest things you see in movies and say," does stuff like that happen." Yes, yes, it does!

So, of course, I had trust issues. The relationship with my father showed me that sometimes when people say they will be right back, you don't see them again for years. I wasn't letting anyone in, and that made me strong. My trust issues were a flashing neon sign that said, I made it here, and I will survive, so, unfortunately, you aren't welcome because you threaten that. I had relationships, but I forced them to remain surface level. The only problem with that is that I truly am not a surface-level person. I am deep, and that is where I dwell. If I wanted to feel like I had a friend, I had to allow them to dive a little deeper. But I was just so afraid.

That is where the warning came from. I would be threatening their life like if I let you in, you better not go anywhere. And for the most part, the ones I did this with were true to their word and remained in my life until we naturally grew apart.

It took opening up to a few people to fully understand that we all have reasons not to trust. I found that I would tell my story, and then the person sitting with me would tell me of their similar past or maybe a different circumstance that I had no idea they were dealing with.

I realized that I gave up the opportunity to connect with others by being shut off because of pain. The fact remains that not everyone you let in will stay, but that is no reason to stay shut off to the world. Because even if it is just for a season, the vulnerability that God can create in that type of human connection can bring such healing. It is the process of realizing that you are not alone, but the pain has been a friend to many. You think you are strong, you hold it all in, but you are terrified and in pain. You show strength when you release the darkness that hides beneath. When you admit to pain, sadness, and loneliness, when you acknowledge that you are in fact in need of connection like all of us, you become strong.

You being closed guarantees that no one will ever prove that they are not like the rest and worthy of being trusted. Here is the thing though, if you have gone this long with your trust issues, then give them to God but also allow him to steer you out of that place. Don't choose for yourself who to let in and open up to because the chances are high that having been shut off for so long, you may not be the best judge of character right now. Let God have a little bit of time to put the right people in your path. Seek him, listen to him, and in time, he will point you in the direction of the people or person that is going to aid him in showing you that some people will truly always have your best interest in mind. If you allow God to plant people in your life, you will find that there are people who will take the time to get to know you and why you are the way you are. Some people will help you carry the heavy things in your life. There will be people that will show up when they say they are going to. There will be people that stay.

But please do release your trust issues. Had I not, I wouldn't have the beautiful relationships that I have right now in my life. I have friendships that I value eternally because they are wrapped around kingdom work, which is exciting. If I hadn't, I wouldn't have the marriage that I have. That alone is worth celebrating every single day. I released my trust issues to God, and then I allowed him to guide me to the person that would never break that new line of trust that he had given me.

TRUST ME. It will be the best decision that you have ever made.

Journal

If you feel like you struggle with trust issues, what do you think that has held you back from?

Have you ever broken someone's trust? What did you do to earn that back?

Action Steps

Even if it has been difficult to trust people, you can always trust God. It helps when you are connected to him. Take some time, get quiet and let God know you trust him with your whole life, all your hopes, and dreams. He will never let you down.

Prayer

Father, right now, I am choosing to trust you and your world. Take away everything that remains in me right now that keeps me from opening up to others and allowing meaningful relationships to enter my life. I believe God that you are going to place divine connections in my life. Connections to people that are going to rebuild my trust. God help me to open up and even be the person that allows others to trust again. Make me vulnerable and strengthen me in that place. Thank you for being trustworthy and for being faithful. I will let you and your faithfulness be the planter of people in my life. I release all of my distrust right now through your power, and I received the people you would have me connect with and the sensitivity to recognize them.

17

SOUL TIES

"Many are confusing love with a soul-tie. The fruit may look similar, but the root is oftentimes very different."—Tony A. Gaskins Jr.

I did a little bit of research to see if I could expand the topics that flowed from me at first and when this one came my way, I knew immediately that it was something that I should write about. Unfortunately, I know all too well the dangers of connecting yourself to someone that is not your spouse. Soul ties are, from my knowledge, a bond that occurs when linking yourself physically to another. Sex is such a powerful connection, whether that is your intention or not. It is by design meant to unify people. That unity strengthens and empowers a marriage, but when sex is outside of the context of marriage, in my opinion, and in layman's terms, it links your issues and creates bondage that you may or may not be aware of.

If you grow up in church and especially as you phase into youth groups, if they try to talk about the things that teens are facing, sex will be a big topic. I know that it was spoken about often in the youth group that I attended. I was told that biblically it is not ok to have sex before you are married. I was taught to try not ever to put myself in that position. I was taught to hold on to my virtue because it is worth waiting for. I was even taught about consequences such as pregnancy and sexually transmitted diseases.

All of that is good and very informative, but one big thing that I was never told about was soul ties. The way you are, connected at a deeper level to any person you give yourself to physically, whether you want to be or not. The connection that causes people to stick around in relationships they are well aware of is not suitable. I call it mad love because it does not love but the infatuation that drives you mad. It's a relationship fueled by jealousy, lust, drama, and a need to fill a deep emptiness.

Sadly any relationship that starts pure and innocent can end up falling into this genre. The moment sex is added to any relationship equation, it becomes increasingly difficult to reason through all couples' challenges. Once you give your body to another, most will fight to keep that connection.

You can also get to the point where you are desensitized, and it no longer affects you so severely because you have had that physical connection with many people. Just because you are desensitized does not mean there is not a negative effect. You have either grown numb to it or have learned to ignore it.

Why does any of this matter?

The problem is that you are now connected with someone that you have no business being linked with. And even if you can move on from that relationship, there is still the residue of that person that resides within you.

The hard part about this is that when it comes time to

connect with the person you have committed your life to, unforeseen challenges will arise.

Although I had taken the time that I felt I needed to seek God and wait for the person I know he had for me, I realized that I had some ties that kept me bound to my past when I married my husband.

I was at first having trouble with intimacy. In the past, shutting off emotions was the best way not to get hurt, but it made it difficult to give my husband all of my life in my marriage.

I wanted more than anything to open up to him every vulnerable place, but the past had taught me that wasn't safe. How could I bind myself to someone entirely if I was still in part tied to another?

I have not done enough study on this topic to dive too deep, and if you feel this is hitting a chord within you, I will encourage you to seek the word and maybe some more reading material that can walk you through this. I just feel like I was warned about all of the surface-level things, but I wasn't told that pieces of my soul would be given when I gave away parts of my body.

Since I was taught that everything will always be in your control, to find out that it wasn't as hard, then to find out someone who took advantage of my naivety was also able to leave behind traces of that ill will, this truly helped me. I felt like I now had the knowledge to explain to anyone why it just isn't worth it to cross that line. I also had guilt leave me once I felt like I knew why something had changed for me after that moment.

I had tied myself to someone who treated sex like a game and treated women like chess pieces. No, I cannot blame him for the choices I made after that, but I believe that a spirit to do the same was then residing in me.

To be able to uproot such a thing allowed me a full release. It allowed me to feel safe again. I no longer felt like sex and relationships were some game that I would forever be playing. I was able to celebrate the victory of the match God made for my husband and me. Most importantly, I was no longer tied to the people I had let the enemy bind me to. I even took it a step further, and I asked God to wipe me clean of the memories. I didn't want to remember the moments I thought were good nor the bad ones. I tried to forget everything, and God was so merciful to grant me that clarity.

Having sex is not just a physical exchange. It's emotional, mental, and spiritual. That is the truth that no one will tell you. That even after only one night, and even if there are no other consequences, there still are soul ties that need to be broken. And the beautiful thing about anyone who finds the strength to wait is that you will be able to enter a marriage knowing that not only are you able to offer your body with no prior physical connections but your soul as well. It's not just the ability to come as a "virgin" and the pride that can swell up around that. It is about coming to your spouse ready to connect soul to soul, knowing this is the first introduction it has had.

What a beautiful thing that could be.

If you think, well, it's too late for that, just like me, ask God to erase every bit of the past, and he will. Your soul deserves a fresh start, and God wants to see you free of those ties.

Journal

Have you had an encounter with someone that you feel has left you damaged?

Once you have gotten rid of the soul ties, in what ways do you think you will be restored?

Action Steps

Ask God if you have any soul ties that need to be severed. Let him show you. If not, pray now for those who need to be released of this specific type of bondage.

Prayer

God, I ask right now that you help me erase any bit of my past that is not pleasing to you. I ask that you purify my heart, my body, and my soul. Make me a new father. I speak in your authority that any unwanted and unwelcome soul tie in my life is broken right now. That is your name I have tied only to you, Jesus. For my current or future spouse, I will be presented without connection to anyone but you father, God, that any residue is lifted and wiped completely clean. I ask that you give me the strength to open myself to you thoroughly and my current or future spouse, knowing that soul ties with you and the man you bring into my life will surely bring you glory. Thank you for your mercy and your grace that has come in and taken away every unwanted thing from my life, including all memories of the past. I am not bound to my past pain or mistakes, but I am made whole and new in you.

MANIPULATION

Manipulation: control or influence (a person or situation) cleverly, unfairly, or unscrupulously.

"Manipulation fueled with good intent can be a blessing. But when used wickedly, it is the beginning of a magician's karmic calamity."—T.F. Hodge

Manipulation is a tool used by people who feel the need to always remain in control. People use manipulation in friendships, relationships, business partnerships, and sometimes people with influence use manipulation to get what they want from people rather than having to come by it themselves.

I dare say manipulation has been used to produce a positive result that a stubborn person refused to understand. As a mother to a toddler, I think manipulation is a tactic that I have to use daily to raise my children and keep my sanity intact.

To uproot manipulation, it is essential to dig deeper under

the surface to find its intention. When it comes to manipulation, the person's intentions behind it are everything. It is their driving force as to why they are using such tactics to remain in control. Maybe someone feels that their intentions are pure, but they use manipulation because there is just fear underneath it all. Fear that they won't be heard out or they won't be understood. Or maybe there is the fear of confrontation. I know I could take this deeper, but it relates so much to things we do as mothers. We try to make something fun, or we give incentives to things because we would like things to happen promptly, and we would also like to avoid it becoming an issue, and there is a scene. In this case, I think a little manipulation because it has the right intentions is not wrong. Now, if you disagree, then we just have different parenting styles, and that is fine. There will be seasons where there is none of that because her comprehension will be at a point of understanding, and it will just come down to me having a conversation.

Let me give you another example of manipulation with pure intention. There was someone in my life who was struggling, and there was not much I could do to reason with the person. They were often offended by suggestions, and even when they would listen, they just never took the advice. I had to sit as a witness to this person claiming they knew how to fix their issues but watching none of their ways work. As time went on, this person became more isolated, got more in-depth into some negative patterns, and was too far away from God to hear in that area. I felt like I had a pretty good idea of the type of lifesaver that this person needed, but I just knew that it wouldn't be received if it came from me. So I manipulated the situation, and I had someone reach out to the person inviting them to join in an area of the church I knew would benefit them. And it was just what was needed. They felt seen by someone other than me. I had become background noise, and I needed someone else to enter stage left and bring a fresh perspective. The person had a complete 180 happen in their life because of my little behind-the-scenes mingling, and I do not regret it at all. My intentions were not out of selfish desire but were to benefit that person's life. I honestly can't even fully take credit for it, God has given me such insight on this person and what their heart needs, and because I was tuned into that wavelength, I had a good idea.

What you have to be able to ask yourself honestly is what are my intentions here? Am I doing these things because I am trying to benefit this person's life, or am I doing these things because I genuinely believe it is best for this person? Typically the ugly side of manipulation where people are genuinely hurt is rooted in one person's selfish desire and extreme need to control.

When you selfishly do things, you are preying on people where they are weak and using that to your advantage. It's like a nasty word, oh that person is manipulative because all along, someone feels as though you are for them, and then it turns out you were for yourself. The worst kind of manipulation is when people use you to get ahead.

It is just like lying because if you are manipulating someone, there is no way around saying that you are deceiving them. Maybe you have gotten through this book, and you feel like you are doing pretty good, and your thinking, wow, Paige, you have issues. But ask yourself, are the people in your life pawns or people? If you organize your life so that all situations and relationships benefit you and that is all that matters, then chances are you are manipulative. I have people in my life that help me a ton, and they are my go-to's in certain areas. And it is beneficial to me, but the reason I feel comfortable doing so is that I am confident that in my way, I am a blessing to them as well. When needed, they know that I will give my absolute all to them because that's who I am.

Manipulation can be subtle, or it can be obvious either way. If it is something that you do, it will begin to affect your relationships. People never want to feel like another person has all of the control because they will ultimately end up pulling away from you.

If you think you may fall into this category, just know that the more genuine and authentic you are, the better your relationships will be and repair any damaged relationship. If you tell people your intentions and desires, you may come off controlling in certain areas, but at least you are honest. In the long term, it will be appreciated. Get a grip on this now. The most difficult lessons in life are all wrapped around the fact that we are not really in control. So let go of the reigns and be pure in all of your dealings with people.

Journal

Have you ever been manipulated?

If so, how did that make you feel?

Now ask yourself, do you tend to be manipulative (regardless of your intentions)?

Action Step

Say what you mean and mean what you say. This week try to be politely straightforward and honest in your dealings with people. Do not use manipulation as a tool to get what you want. This will help you diagnose how often, if ever, you were manipulative.

Parents, this excludes you and your dealing with the children.

Prayer

Help me to slow down God and evaluate my intentions behind everything that I do. I want to be confident that I am not ruling people or treating them as pawns in my master plan. Help me to let go of control and of the things that I cannot control. Give me the wisdom to know what lines not to cross and help me do nothing out of selfish desire. Thank you for purifying me and my intentions.

19

ANGER

An intense negative emotion ranging from mild irritation to rage.

"A heart filled with anger has no room for love."—Joan Lunden

Unfortunately, anger is another thing that I know all too well. So congratulations to all of you for benefitting from all of my issues. Also, praise God that he can rescue us not just from one thing but from all things. As you can tell from this book, I like to find the root of things. I want to look back at my life and try to pinpoint when and why specific issues in my life arose.

So as far as anger, I don't know that I could tell you that. I know that I am a type-A personality, which typically is very obvious even at a young age. When I didn't get my way, I would throw some severe fits. So much so that my family made up and would sing a song about it.

Oh, she's bad Charlie Allessandra Paige, Baddest girl when she's in a rage.

Better put her in a cage, Charlie Allessandra Paige.

That makes me laugh to think about, but I am sure my mom didn't find it all that funny. Then fast forward into my teen years and what it turned into definitely wasn't funny. I got into a handful of fights in high school and walked away with handfuls of hair missing from my head. One fight got me a nice little suspension. Another my mom just took me out of school for a week just because I needed a break. Yeah, I was sad about some girl drama, but the rage portion of that dilemma led to me throwing a science book at a girl's head in the middle of class. My mom took me out, and I didn't get kicked out because the science teacher vouched for me. He told the principal he may have done the same thing hearing what the girls were saying but still, it was not ok.

That kind of anger leads to outbursts of rage that are hard to control, and heaven forbid you injure someone in a way that you cannot take back for some temporary anger over words.

It wasn't just that I wanted to be the tough girl. I wasn't trying to look cool or have that persona. I couldn't process ill-treatment of any kind. Not from my peers, not from teachers, not from anyone. I didn't process things well, and there was no time for that, and I REACTED to everything. This would affect my friendships, relationships and affect jobs that I had in the future. Out of anger, I always said whatever I thought. There was so much immaturity in that, but I was just an angry young girl.

I thought that many things in life were unfair, and that made me mad. I thought it was unfair that my dad left. It was unfair that my mom had to take care of us on her own. It was unfair that my grandma died of cancer. It was unfair that a boy manipulated me and took advantage of me when I was too young. It was unfair that I didn't have a ton of money like many of the kids I went to school with. It was unfair that I felt less than everyone around me.

Anger and rage can be so much more than this. This is just my experience. Maybe you have had so much of it in your life that it has affected you. Perhaps you have seen consequences because of it. The most I have gotten was a car ride home when I was in third grade in the back of a police car because I fought a girl that wouldn't let me jump on her trampoline. To which my mom just had nothing to say.

Maybe you have hurt someone, or hurt yourself, or you have done or said something that you can't take back because you were so blinded by anger.

That is a hard place to be, to feel like you have no control of your own emotions. I have been there. I have had anger and rage uprooted, and that was not easily done. Anger and rage tend to dig their claws in deep so that it just rests somewhere you can't see it until you blow up. Having fits of rage can even surprise you.

This is something that I knew I needed to make sure that I had under control before I had kids. I didn't want them to receive my outbursts for doing little things that honestly didn't matter. I didn't want to be the mom that freaked out over spilled milk.

For all things, I turn to God, I dig into scriptures, and I receive prayer from the people I trust. Then I try to learn something that can be applied.

I learned the importance of becoming a responder and not a reactor. When you react in situations, you don't take time to think and process things. You just immediately flow into a counterattack. At this point, you don't even know why it is that you are so angry. You are not even going to be able to accurately articulate what hurt you. You are just going to launch some hurtful comments and even potentially actions because you have not even thought about it.

I look back at so many situations where I just reacted, and It flat out makes me embarrassed. The worst is when you didn't have the time to gain clarity, you get all angry about something that maybe you wholly misunderstood. You feel so stupid when you realize that you either took something out of context or just heard something altogether wrong. But even if you heard right to react usually means that you overreact. And no matter how justified you are, overreacting just isn't cute.

If you slow down and take the time to process things, you can decide the best way to respond to something. Maybe that means that you just need to ask for clarity on something or just ask if that is what the person meant to say or do. That can typically create the proper dialogue to just figure things out without getting upset. At this moment, without getting emotions involved, you have the opportunity to let the person know how it is that you received what they said or did and how that made you feel. Unless something negative was intentionally done (and if so, you need to evaluate if this person should be in your life), then, for the most part, they are going to be appalled that they made you feel that way. As soon as I know someone's intentions were not to hurt me, I automatically feel better. Then it is just a matter of resolving things and moving on.

This is something that you want to put in place when you work with people. The chances are that in your office there are people that maybe you don't get along the best with. If you are a reactor, you will have an agitated work environment, and it is just not worth it. Some people you just can't reason with even if you are a responder, and so those are the people that you simply must ignore. Ignoring things takes a skill set. Especially when the things that they are doing are making your blood boil. Eventually, you will realize it doesn't matter, and you will let it go. If you don't ignore and you react, then it will cause constant issues for you.

Do you realize that some people live for that kind of thing? Some people will say and do the craziest things because they are looking to get a rise out of you. Nothing will change on their end if they succeed, but you will be embarrassed for how you acted. I feel like people mostly like to do this with proclaimed Christians. It's like they want to prove that we are just as messed up as they are. Although we might be and we have some things to work on like everyone, just don't give the person the satisfaction of proving that to be true. Instead, choose to take the high road. You will have a more significant opportunity to witness to people if later you can say, yeah, that drove me crazy, but I chose not to let it bother me, with the help of Jesus.

This is so my dad. He will reach out and reach out with no response because he is not a part of my life. Then he will say some horrible things and cause me to flip my lid. After, I will react, and I realize that he just wanted to get a rise out of me. Because oddly enough, it is better for him to feel hated rather than ignored. When he is hated, he can justify himself and say they aren't any better than me. When he is ignored, he blames himself and probably realizes that it is actually on him and needs to change. I don't know about you, but I don't want my short-sided anger to permit him to let himself off the hook.

You can stop letting anger rule your life right now. Stop letting anger win battles because any battle won in anger is lost in the sight of God.

Journal

Do you struggle with anger?

Do you feel like you can recognize your triggers?

Action Steps

- If you find yourself getting angry this week, take a step back and look at why.
- Choose a way to release the anger you feel like working out!

Prayer

Jesus, I just that you take me over right now. Remove any of the residues of anger and rage inside of me. I don't care where it came from. I just have no room for it in my life anymore. I want to operate in the fruits of your spirit, lord. I don't want to be a reactor, and I don't want to be angry anymore. Uproot all of it right now, Jesus, and I will do my part to keep it out of my heart. Let your fullness and joy fill every void, and every dark place there once was in me.

20

TRAGIC LOSS

Little by little, we let go of loss, but never of Love.

I believe that the things that we face in life directly reflect who we become. I think dealing with the ups and downs, the good and not good, these things shape us. Sometimes we allow the things we face to change us for the better, and sometimes we allow the things that change us to shape us into the worst version of ourselves.

I would even venture to say that whichever way you go, the change may not be intentional, but it was just the way you dealt with your circumstances.

Even if it affects you for the worse, no matter how far you go, you can still decide to take everything you know and make the most out of it. That you can turn any dark situation and any negative path you have gone down into a street of silver lining. On this path, you choose to take the route that exposes the pain and confronts it head-on. This route is undoubtedly the more challenging route, but it comes with the reward of overcoming your circumstances.

In this life, there are so many things that we face. Some things are not our fault and are out of our control. Then there are the moments when you're sitting in poop, and you realized you made the choices that led to that very smelly moment in your life, and there is nothing you can do but take a big whiff to burn the stench of that decision into your mid.

Then there are the things that happen that we cannot account for at all, the moments that bring such unbearable pain, and no one can give you an answer as to why. These moments are the makers or breakers. The moments I am referring to are the tragic loss of loved ones. Whether it was something unforeseen or sickness that took someone too soon, these are the pains that hurt beyond comprehension.

Some people have felt this pain more than once in a lifetime, and ultimately most of us will eventually. Then some have never felt it and praise God for that. And then you might be the one living in fear of that outcome because of the constant thought of your loved one that has been given an unfair and unencouraging diagnosis.

There is not much that can make a human begin to ask questions of the universe and mainly of God than when a loved one is ripped from our arms. This is why I feel so strongly about the loss being one of the more defining moments in someone's life.

You can come away angry, broken, emotionless, ill, suicidal, in need of revenge, in need of answers, seeking relief, seeking solace, seeking quiet, or seeking loud. The main thing is that a piece of you seems to have left for good, and you have no idea how on earth you are ever going to get that back.

Then to make matters worse, you have very well-meaning

people telling you "it was just their time," "they are in a better place," "God just needed them," and so on. I find it best practice to avoid such statements that attempt to justify something utterly unjustifiable, especially by some nonsense blanket statement like that.

I am sorry, but no one wants to be told that their loved one is better off anywhere other than in their arms. No one wants to be told that their loved one who was taken by a sickness, whether young or old, was taken because it was just time for them to go, not when there were things left undone and memories left to create.

But please, oh, please don't tell someone that God took their loved one from them. There is nothing as quiet as confusing as the claim that God is a healer and God is good but then also to say that he is the one that took them from you.

Some things happen that are not good on this earth, and those things are no God's doing. This seems to go against the word, but I want to offer you a scenario that might clarify what I am trying to say. This perspective comes from a blog that I had written a few years back.

I wrote this a while back with someone specific on my heart, someone experiencing inexplicable loss. When I messaged them with more prayers and extra condolences, they did not understand why God took their loved one from them. I was so disheartened that someone could believe that, so I wrote this. I got confirmation on sharing it this weekend at a women's conference when several people mentioned this specifically. I hope this encourages someone dealing with loss and helps them to know that God is not to blame.

For Peaches & the one Who called her that

People often fall under the misconception that because God is a receiver of those we dearly loved and have lost, he is also the taker.

Some are at peace with this notion because they believe that God is good and that there must be some reason for this, some bigger plan that we just aren't aware of. And then there are a lot of people that become angry with God and confused because of this.

But consider this...

What if we got frustrated and angry with foster parents. Or we were confused and questioned the intentions of the ones the proceed towards adoption. What if we considered them the takers for being willing to receive those who needed a home because their current situation is no longer safe or liveable. Don't we typically commend them for their heroism; don't we applaud them for their selflessness? Do we blame them for the things that happened before the children arrived in their care?

The answer is no, at least from my perspective. Maybe you have witnessed or experienced otherwise. But for the most part, we encourage and offer praise to the parents brave enough to adopt and foster. We celebrate them for all that they are doing to help a child heal. We say things like, "I don't know how you do what you are doing, especially with children that aren't your own." We are in shock and awe of someone who chooses to take responsibility for the ones that no one else was. Then we are in complete amazement when people take on the tough cases, taking on the responsibility of correcting someone else's mistakes.

My greatest desire is for people to start looking at my best friend, My Father in Heaven, that way. That they see him through that same lens, in awe of the things he is willing to do for his children. We live in a fallen world, and there are so much death and destruction that he is not responsible for. There are times when this world is just not livable anymore for someone. When disease plagues the life of someone innocent, someone who has done nothing *wrong, I challenge you to try and view God in this situation differently.*

It is never his will for someone to be sick or for tragedy to show up on your doorstep randomly. He is the Hero of the story, not the villain. He is the Foster parent that always moves for permanent residence in his house where he knows he can look after you best. He is the one who receives a person when this world is just no longer a good home. God swings his door wide open and says, "Come on in."

Unfortunately, when people try to comfort people who have had someone taken from their lives, they sometimes mistakenly verbalize it incorrectly. They don't realize that when someone is hurting typically, what they hear is that God is to blame. "God wanted to bring his Angel home" and all the other sentiments that are often said in the ears of the hurting at funeral homes. But God is not to blame for the chaos that happens to us in this life, but he shows up when he doesn't have to and takes on the responsibility of righting the wrongs that weren't his own.

If you have lost someone, be comforted that God has found them but don't be deceived into thinking he is the one that took them away.

I hope and pray that after reading that perspective, you can breathe in some freedom. If you have been negatively affected by a tragic loss because of a skewed view of God, I genuinely hope this speaks to you. It is your choice on how this loss defines your life. Will you allow the loss that we all eventually experience in this life to control your future and steal your joy. Or will you claim victory over death and choose to live on the other side of that pain. In a place where your heart can miss someone so profoundly, but your optimism remains untainted?

Let me tell you this one last thing. If the person you lost

loved you as much as you loved them, then I guarantee that no ounce of that person wants you to allow pain to control your life. If anything, maybe there are things that they would like for you to finish for them. For me, there was no doubt that my grandmother wanted me to be happy, and she wanted me to accomplish big things. And there were several moments when I knew I was making bad decisions and just the thought of her had me wanting to make things right. I want more than anything to carry with me a piece of her strong-willed and stubborn personality. I want to be a woman of God that loves and serves my community and, above all, my family. I want to be vocal on the things I believe in as she was because then, to me, it's like she never really left. After all, she remains in me.

Psalm 34:18 says The Lord is close to the brokenhearted and saves those who are crushed in spirit.

God is right there waiting to heal and to mend your broken heart, to lift you when the pain of loss threatens your joy. Lift your eyes to him, and you will see there is so much more than this life. This place is temporary, but there is a new life, an eternal life, and seeing people finish their race and when their prize is something to be rejoicing about, and God will help you to see that.

Journal

Have you experienced an impactful loss in your life?

Where are you in the grieving process, and how have you allowed God to help?

If you haven't, how do you plan to?

Action Steps

- Tell someone a story about the loved one you lost, I know this may seem like a painful task, but this keeps them alive in you. The pieces that they left behind come to life in their memory, and it has a beautiful way of making you feel connected once again. God gave stories and memories that power. After all, how else were his believers supposed to share the good news?

Prayer

Father, thank you for being the good Father that you are. Thank you for being the father who doesn't take but instead received your children who this fallen world has broken. Thank you for being willing to accept even though you may be blamed for that. I just ask that right now, you strengthen me in the knowledge that you are a good good father; that is who you are and who you always will be. I ask that you forgive me of doubt and the ways I have blamed you for my pain. I know that in you, I will find the answers to the questions my soul is seeking. I know that you have not failed, and I am sorry if I had lost my faith in your wonder-working power. Heal me right now, God, bring comfort and peace to my soul. Let me take this circumstance and allow good to come from it, God. That may seem impossible that I could take this tragedy and, with your help, have it become a testimony. But with you, there are no impossibilities.

21

PRIDE

Pride: a feeling or deep pleasure or satisfaction derived from one's achievements, the achievements of those with whom one is closely associated, or from qualities or possessions that are widely admired.

Pride will always be the longest distance between two people.

Darling, Pride cometh before the falleth. Not to get all old English on you, but this was, is, and will always be one of the statements you can live by. The moment that you think you are pretty cool and you begin to read your press clippings, your friend is getting dangerously close to getting knocked down to size. This is the way life is. It just shows you that you are not invincible, your poop does stink, and you are not the end all be all that you either are thinking or acting like you are. Not to say that you aren't amazing, don't get me wrong. Nor am I saying that it isn't okay to display confidence. The problem comes when you begin to view yourself as better than anyone else.

There is a difference between being proud of yourself and full of yourself. The moment you feel super proud of yourself should be the moment where you do a self-check and keep your head down to stay behind that line. If you flirt too closely to this line, then what will happen is you will be presented with an opportunity to be humble, and when you are riding that line, it's difficult not to cross it. Instead of being humble and making that choice on your own, you will be humbled, which does not feel good.

Every opportunity in which God allows you to rise is an opportunity for you to point the Glory back to the one who truly deserves it, to tell the true story of your success. If you're anything like me, the truth is that for some reason, God blesses me. When all the lights are shining in your direction, all eyes and ears are yours. It is so tricky because you feel fantastic at that moment; you start to think you earned it because you are awesome. Just don't forget that you are not the one that got you there. That would be similar to attending your 50th wedding anniversary. Everyone is celebrating the beautiful life that you and your husband have built together, and of course, they want to hear from you. You get the microphone, and you politely greet all of your friends and family. In your speech, you say how hard you worked to be the best wife you could be. You list off all of your attributes, accolades, accomplishments as a wife and then as a mother, and everything you contributed to the relationship. You say all of this without admitting to the simple fact that if it weren't for the love and the grace of your husband or the power and presence of God in your marriage, then you wouldn't be there.

Being prideful is like thinking the reasoning behind why anything you do is successful is just because you are involved. I guess you could call it a superiority complex or even a God complex. The reason I say that is because then you get the praises from others. They begin to think you have what you have because there is something about you, some quality they need to work towards. You are getting the Glory that God deserves. He created us to glorify him. It is the one thing that he cannot do for himself. Self-edification is just embarrassing. So when we have an opportunity to give God all of the glory and be humble in moments of the spotlight, we take all of the credit for ourselves, and we are operating outside of our design.

Of course, I know this from personal experience. I don't know if it was a defense mechanism or what, but I walked into my early 20's just feeling like I was God's gift to the world. I felt like I could say and do whatever I wanted, and people should just be thankful to know me. I also knew that everything I would try to do would succeed because I was special, and I was meant for greatness. I knew that all these other people had to work at everything, but everything would just work for me. High hopes were not the issue. I was a dreamer with an entitlement mentality because I was so unbelievably prideful. I always thought I was right, and I would shut you down if you disagreed with my opinion. I was the worst, honestly. If you knew me then and you are still my friend, well, God bless your darling soul, and you deserve all of the blessings.

I was trying to become a better person, but even my husband came into my life when I hadn't yet been brought down to earth. The good thing about him is he doesn't get easily influenced, he is not easily offended, and he would ignore my antics, more or less.

I met success even in my prideful season, but because of that, I quickly met failure. I went from this tall tower down in the slumps because I had to be taught so many little things. These lessons were not to make me feel insignificant. The lessons reminded me that I was significant, but so was everyone else. I was taught how to appreciate people at a high level because without others' help, you will get nowhere, and if you do make it without the use of others, you will be lonely at the top. I had to learn that I didn't know everything, I wasn't good at everything, and just because I thought it would work didn't mean it would. I was shown, though, that there were people who knew what I didn't, they could do what I couldn't, and if I had an idea then working with others, I am much more likely to accomplish it.

I had to learn that I had begun to hold my value and identity in whether I got the applause, which made me realize that I was performing. I wasn't living and fighting for what mattered. My value could not be wrapped up in whether I was getting the attention or approval from others to be happy long term. I had to build myself up in God and be confident in myself no matter what season I found myself in, desert or promise.

Although God fiercely loves me, I learned that I am not exempt from his correction if I am behaving like a fool. The worst part about being a prideful person is that there is a tendency to belittle others that they feel are below them. I had to be brought down to earth to realize that I am above no one. No measure of success ever permits you to trample on the people that God has called you to love, to lead, and to aid in their growth. How can you grow something that you trample on?

For me, the main lesson to my pride was that I am brilliant and talented, but also so is everyone in their way. I need to focus on making sure that I don't waste the gifts given to me, and I need to worry far less about what other people are doing with theirs or what they think of mine. I needed to grow in my ability to recognize others' gifts and help God by being someone who encourages others to be fruitful in those things. Helping cultivate other's gifts helped me see on a larger scale the gifted brilliance he planted in his children. This put me in my place but in the best way because I then just begin to see my giftings as pieces to the much bigger puzzle. The final result needs my pieces but only as much as it needs yours. I have never felt a more profound sense of community than I do now as I am deeply ingrained in seeing other people's passions come to life as I am simultaneously applying God's resurrection power to mine.

If you feel like you have many good things going on in your life, but you feel more lonely than ever, you may want to check your pride. Prideful people push others away because they spew the message that they don't need anyone and they are good all by themselves.

Maybe you are trying to figure out how to control that pride because it wells up inside you involuntarily. Perhaps your Pride is a defense mechanism for you feeling utterly unqualified, so you let that arrogance rise inside you because that is better than feeling unworthy. There is no need to hide what you are truly feeling. God can do more through your weakness than he ever could in your place of "strength." When you admit to being weak and feeling less than, instead of trying to be the one to build yourself up, let God have a go of it. If he does the work, he will strengthen who you are in him, which automatically cancels that unworthy feeling.

James 4:10: Humble yourselves before the Lord, and he will lift you.

You may feel like I did, that you have to hold your head high and lift yourself because no one else will do that for you. That stems from a place of disappointment, where you just don't get the recognition or affirmation that you feel you need. To humble yourself seems to be a bad thing. It looks like you have to make yourself lowly and go back to the dirt that has been calling you your whole life. That is just not what God is asking of you. He wants you to entirely rely on him and trust in him instead of yourself. He will lift you. He is not one to break his word. No promotion could be better than the promotion that God plans to give you when you allow that humbling in your life.

Journal

Have you ever been through a season of humbling? What did
you learn in that season?

How has your pride affected you?

In what areas of your life do you notice yourself becoming
prideful now?

Action Steps

- Be sure and be intentional about giving God the Glory today. Any chance you get, point the credit of any good thing back to God.

Prayer

God, we just give our lives fully over to you, not in some things but all things. We lower ourselves before you, knowing that things are so much better your way. We are tired of trying to do things in our strength, tired of trying to raise ourselves. Lord, we need you to take us in all our brokenness, mold us, and make us into something worthy of representing your name. Forgive me for my prideful way, and forgive me if that pride has been damaging to anyone else. I ask for that correction daily, God, so that I can be the type of humble servant worthy of an assignment from you. I long to bring you Glory, and I have failed in that, but I ask for another chance like you did with Peter God, give me another opportunity to represent your name and your kingdom knowing yours is the power.

Amen!

22

ANXIETY

A feeling of worry, nervousness, or unease, typically about an imminent event or something with an uncertain outcome.

"Our Anxiety does not empty tomorrow of its sorrows, but only empties today of its strengths." —Charles H. Spurgeon

I f you know me, there may be several topics in this book that I speak of having personally dealt with, and some I have never even really heard me talk about them. But if there is one victory in my life that I talk about all the time, it is my past and current triumph over anxiety.

I say current because although you can conquer the beast of anxiety, I feel it is something you must fight to keep off for the rest of your life. When you know the tools and you know the triggers, this can be easily done.

Anxiety was getting the best of me for so long because I never sought to understand what was going on with me. I was never officially diagnosed, and therefore I lived with it for so long, thinking this was just the way I am.

In hindsight, I am glad I didn't go the medical route and get a diagnosis to get on medication potentially. I don't say that because I think there is anything wrong with that way, but looking back, I am thankful for the way my journey unfolded. When I was confronted with the fact that I was dealing with pretty severe anxiety, I was forced to face it head-on with God at my side. I was diagnosed by reality and prescribed a cure with Jesus and Joyce Meyer at my side.

I had a book called the pursuit of peace sitting in my nightstand drawer for years. It was something that I had plans to read someday. The main reason is that being the strong woman I am just didn't think I would relate much to it. (I laugh when I think about the false strength that I was operating in). The subtitle just threw me off; "how to conquer worry, doubt, anxiety, and fear." I was one of those who never wanted to let on that there was anything wrong with me, so what would I look like reading that book. Then my husband might know the dirty secret I keep inside, that deep down, I think I might genuinely be crazy.

I had just been so jaded by so many people in my life who complained about having anxiety and let it be an excuse for, pardon my language but having a piss poor attitude all of the time. I struggled with so many things, but I was bound and determined not to let "my demons" affect the people around me. That is what my dad did to everyone in his life, and I didn't want to be that person. He had a victim mentality, and he blamed his father for how he treated us and for the demons he allowed to rule his life. The last thing that I wanted was to repeat that cycle.

I remember my mom asking me one time in the car if I thought I needed to see a therapist. Instead of telling her yes, I realized I had led on a little too much to my internal struggle, so I needed to suck it up and play pretend. I would rather just admit to my mistakes and take personal responsibility for being an idiot and making poor choices than worry her by telling her how much I was struggling.

This is so dangerous, but sadly it is what so many people do. So I am not against going to a doctor to find out some answers because it is much better than suffering in silence. I happen to believe as a culture, we should normalize therapy, if for no reason other than learning how to communicate our feelings. Frankly, it would have been nice for me to find out with some assistance that there was a reason behind the patterns of poor behavior that I seemed to have zero control over. I shouldn't have been fighting so hard to control myself but rather learn myself and understand why.

I am just glad that I found the resources that I did, and it never got so bad that it affected those around me. My family would have never forgiven themselves if I had let myself go to those deeper and darker places that anxiety can take you because they truly wouldn't have known how bad it was.

Eventually, I got to this place in my life where I needed change. Honestly, I was desperate. I was so sick and tired of all of the swirling thoughts that just wouldn't let me be. I was so sick of worrying for the sake of worrying. I was sick of not being able to sleep at night and being tormented by thoughts and fears. I was even angrier that those thoughts would carry over into my sleep, creating wild dreams that left me feeling restless in the morning when it was time to peel myself out of bed.

I was tired of how all of this affected my attitude and my action, which would affect all of my relationships in the long run. I felt as though I was losing myself, and I didn't know what to do.

This was all the while sustaining what I thought was a strong relationship with God pursuing the path that I believed he had me on. This wasn't while I was at the same time living a life of sin, no my anxiety came with me, and I was actually in a place where to everyone else, it appeared I had my act together. Things just aren't adding up, and I knew I needed something to change.

I went to a bible study at my sister's house, where the Pastors of her church came to speak. I was so hungry for change that I was willing to go the extra mile for answers.

I remember at the end, they let people know that if they wanted prayer, they would be happy to pray with them. So I received prayer from the Pastor's wife. From that moment on, things in my life would be different. She began to pray, and I thought she would speak some lovely things over me and I would be on a spiritual high, but instead, she went to battle. She spoke a silence to all of the voices in my head. Even though she was speaking quietly into my ear for a moment, I allowed worry to rise. That worry told me to be afraid that someone may have heard her and would now know my secret. I had to fight to poke my head out from behind the worry that stood between us at that moment because my spirit knew the truth. So she kept going, and I let it all come in. It was like washing and cleansing of my mind that I needed. For the first time, the chaos in my mind was brought to light, and because of that, anxiety no longer had a place to hide. Without it hidden, it was much easier to face head-on.

All of a sudden, it was like all of the junk in my mind had yielded to the spirit. There was a cease-fire, and it was effective. But I knew that if I was not proactive, this wouldn't last forever.

I knew that I had to take that moment to rid myself of this issue in my life entirely.

So I went home. I opened my nightstand drawer. And I opened that book.

As I began to read, I felt like the book had been written about me. I finally confirmed through reading about the anxiety just how accurate my self-diagnosis was. It was uncanny how much I related to all of the stories and examples. Just like that, I was on the road to recovery.

Even though I felt like she was talking to me about me, I knew these were stories of her experiences and of people she had worked with. Just these examples made me feel less alone and less crazy. I finally felt like there might be some answers to the constant mental torment that I was in.

One of the most helpful things from this book for me was finding out some boundaries to begin to install in my life that would greatly diminish the anxiety that I was bringing on myself. Finding out something as simple as being late was causing me to be anxious and making things way harder than they needed to be. I started to decide what I would wear to events ahead of time, so that was one less thing I had to do as I got ready. I also allowed an extra 30 minutes into my process to make up for the potential of traffic or other things outside of my control. I even stopped speeding, which eliminated the anxiety of looking for police officers around every corner. It helped that I was no longer already running late. This is one example of the many, but wow, how helpful this little tweak was. Who knew poor time management was a contributing factor to my daily insanity.

This book and the referenced scriptures were my manuals for the next six months of my life. I am not one of those who can speed read anyway. I like to take my time to digest what I am reading. But with this book, I slowed way down, and I took it all in. There wasn't a single chapter that wasn't rich with great advice and things that I knew I needed to do. I would read and fully comprehend, and then I would put together action plans for applying these things to my life.

The gut feeling of anxiousness continued to diminish until finally it was gone, and the only time it would reappear was the night before big trips and, of course, Christmas. Admittedly I am still like a child in this way where I get so excited and anxious I can hardly sleep before big days. I can deal with that, but Walking around with that constant feeling in my gut didn't feel like excitement. It felt like torture.

I remember when my husband would say things like "relax" or "chill out" because I was just always so tense, so worried, and trying to draw these deep breaths to calm myself down. He learned not to say those two phrases because they were as offensive to me as calling me out of my name. It was frustrating to be told to calm down when you so desperately want to, and you just don't know-how.

Now calm is an essential part of my life.

In the past, I craved peace like you crave water in the desert heat. It was my number one prayer and petition to the lord. When it was spoken of in the word or sung about, my mouth would water. Oh, to know that feeling. Then when I exhaled all of those concerns and fears and all of the anxiousness, I was finally able to inhale the spirit of the Lord that flooded me with peace shalom. If you know me, when I say bye to people, I say peace shalom. Which is saying peace twice, and I love that. Peace on peace is with you, my friend, because man, that feels good. The real peace of the Lord is better than any legal or illegal high that you can get. Trust me. I have tried.

Once I had peace infiltrate my life, I was just able to think more clearly and rationally. I realized that though not everything was under my control, I needed many things to change, which would greatly benefit my situation. Before, everything was so out of my control. I thought that meant that everyone else was to blame, and that was far from the truth. I was able to change the way that I viewed things and the way I handled situations. I was able to reason with myself when the uncontrollable occurred. I was able to process negative or chaotic situations and find solutions.

Once I tackled anxiety, literally, everything in my life got better. Believe me when I say that you can have victory over anxiety, but it doesn't come without work. You must work with God to rid yourself of anxiety and earn a life of peace.

Psalm 34:4: "I sought the Lord. He answered me; he delivered me from all my fears."

To know that I alone cannot conquer the things that trouble me but that in a moment when I pray, he hears me and he will answer me, just that knowledge sends peace over me like a cool water. If I am doing all the little things not to be anxious and I feel I am fighting a losing battle, I need to seek the Lord, and he will answer me.

Journal

Are you struggling with anxious thoughts? Is this a new thing or something you have dealt with for a long time?

Tell me what gets you worked up the most.

Now let's rewrite the narrative. Imagine yourself obsessively thinking about a topic once again, but then as often as you can speaking, but GOD IS IN CONTROL. Eventually, you will believe that and begin to surrender.

Action steps

- Find a fellow believer that will pray with you and help you call out your anxious thoughts and pray peace like a flood over your mind!

Prayer

Jesus, I just give all of my heaviness to you right now. I lay all of it down at your feet. I surrender it all to you lord, I don't want to control it, and I no longer wish to carry it. I need you to be my peace, Lord. Holy Spirit, come right now and invade my life. I speak a silence to all chatter that is not of God, and I declare that my mind is a place of peace and clarity. God, you are the master of my life, which means I have nothing to worry about, and there is nothing and no one I should fear. I breathe you in right now, and I will leave every bit of that anxiousness behind me, and every day I will live and breathe and rest in you. In Jesus' name.

*If this chapter was a hot button for you, I plan to write a whole book on this topic one day. For now, Joyce has that covered. Go pick up a copy of *The Pursuit of Peace*. I can guarantee that you will be changed if you dive into it the way that I did.

23

COPYING

"Make a similar or identical version of: reproduce. Imitate the style or behavior of You cannot innovate by copying." —Larry Ellison

This one will be quick. And honestly, I added this here for personal reasons, I don't know if that is right or wrong, but it is what it is. Out of all of these roots that entangle us, this is one that I have not personally struggled with until more recently. While writing this book, I was tempted to sugarcoat some of the content to match the writing style that is trending right now. Although my intention is not to be popular, rather to be useful, I still, because of comparison, almost became a copycat. I almost became one of my biggest pet peeves by not living in my authenticity and going with a style that seemed to be working. I would be so annoyed by anyone jockeying my style, but I was so tempted to be that person.

I have just always been this very original person, and I wanted to be that way. I have always wanted to express myself creatively without the threat that someone would take my ideas. That happened all too often, especially in high school.

Even though seasons of really wanting to fit in, I wanted it to be because people got to know me and accepted me for who I was, not because I changed myself to fit some mold. I didn't want to be like everyone else, but I also didn't want to be excluded by everyone either.

I added this topic because what I was so resistant to in high school I might not have been if I had been confronted with social media the way young people are these days. It is hard for people to be original in a world where what others think is cool is continually being put in front of your face. Not only can you see what people like, but you can also see what they don't by the lack of likes.

Maybe I would have tried out a new outfit that was different than what everyone else was wearing, but then I would have been immediately aware of how other people felt about it via social media. I can be honest with myself and say that I have as an adult struggled with this more than I did as a teenager because of social media.

Even those who have original thoughts, their content is taken, which turns into a trending topic that everyone gets to talk about with no credit to the first person to step out. Being original can very quickly become unoriginal, and that can be very disheartening. It is also challenging to stay in your lane of creativity and choose to be innovative when you see something working so well for another.

So what about you, friend? How much of your life and your truth are you living. How much of the life you live day to day is out of the habit of copying and pasting others' ideas and thoughts.

Or let's go even deeper because, as you know, that is my

favorite thing to do. Are you currently living your life in a way that is genuinely you, deep down to the core, all the way to the way you are dressing? Or are you doing things, trying to be someone that you think others will like more. Have you copied and pasted another image to be the girl you think your significant other wants? Or to be the girl that your friends think you should be?

Sometimes copying isn't to fit in as much as it is to feel loved by the people that you are afraid won't like you for who you are. Maybe you dress down because perhaps if you expressed yourself, it would be too much for the people in your life, and they would want you to tone it down. Maybe you dress up and add flair that isn't you, but you do so because it is trendy, and your deepest fear is that you are a bore to those around you.

The people that truly know you and love you would never ask you to change or do something that is not you for the sake of fitting in. They will be able to spot the counterfeit in you, and they will either think they don't know you that well or wonder who you are trying to please.

You may end up damaging the real relationships in your life when you attempt to be something that you are not, and that is the last thing that anyone wants.

So let me just share with you my signature line. The moment I heard it, I loved it, and I knew that I would carry it with me for the rest of my life. I knew that it would be a reminder to myself and those around me to be true to themselves.

"Don't be like the rest of them, Darling."

I just love that! Don't try to be like anyone but you. Don't do what everyone else does and conform to fit in. It is boring, and it is never worth it. You don't want to look back at your life and realize that you never truly let yourself live because you never really figured out who you were. Don't let people change you because those that want to are temporary anyways. You are priceless and 100% unique. The way your mind works, how your heart feels, the things you like, and the things you are good at. All of these things are unique to you and only you.

More than that, inside of you is a lot of good stuff that you were meant to protect, to grow, to cultivate, and then to give out to the world. That is why you are here, to give to the world the beauty that is within you. The world could use more beauty, and it is waiting for yours.

You are more beautiful right now at this moment than you even know. You are smarter than you think you are, capable of absolutely anything you put your mind to. You are a rare gem that others are out there searching for, just hoping to one day encounter someone genuine and authentic. You are a treasure to your heavenly father, and if you let him, he will take what is different about you and expand it, creating a life that you couldn't dream up if you tried.

Trust me, although I feel like I am just getting started, I am living this right now. Because I choose to love the me that God created and because I let him create through me, I experience an unbounded Joy. When I look at myself in the mirror, I can say without a doubt that I am who I am supposed to be, and I have stolen no one's identity or destiny. I can smile and say I love me.

Ephesians 2:10 You are God's masterpiece.

No one can do what you do, so don't get stuck in a life forgetting how wonderfully unique you are and copying everyone around you. When you do that, you deprive the world of the gift of you.

Journal

Which end of copying do you find yourself on, Frequently copying others or always being the one who is being copied?

Do you recognize the things that make you unique and valuable? If so, write them out.

Action Steps

- Reach out to a close friend or even a few and ask them to tell you what your strengths are and, in their eyes, what makes you unique. (Typically, others see our value in ways that we cannot).

Dare

I dare you to be even bolder and available to some potential correction by asking in what ways do you think I sometimes tend to be unoriginal. Use their feedback to challenge you in new areas!

Prayer

Creator of the universe and designer of my life, I am so in awe of all of your beautiful works. I am even more in awe that you took the time to make me different. You slowed down and perfected me to be the very best me I could be, and I am so thankful for that. God help me strip away every single false layer that I have applied, thus covering up your unique design. Help me take out the things I have added that are counterfeit and only aid in hiding the real me. I want to shine for you, Jesus, so help me see what you see when you look at me. Help me to know through your word my real value. Help me stand firm, holding nothing of myself back but giving the world what they can only get from me.

24

ATTENTION SEEKING

Someone who acts solely in a way that is geared towards garnering the attention of other people. The attention they get makes them feel better about themselves, boosts their self-esteem, and doesn't matter if that attention is good or bad.

People who shine from within don't need the spotlight.

Attention seeking may seem reserved for the teenage girl struggling to find herself, but if we all just keep it real, we know we took some of those tactics with us into our adult lives. Attention is something everyone desires and craves.

Now everywhere I go, I see this being the primary way people live their lives and make choices. I mean, just one trip to your local gym will be proof enough that there are so many people who are in desperate need of others' attention. I mean, honestly, why else would you make yoga-type moves in the middle of a weight lifting area while wearing panties and a bralette. This is truly an alarming sight that I have seen too many times. I would have felt judgmental and thrown severe shade in the past, but now I just find myself hurting for them. I just want to walk up to the girl and find some way to encourage her because, more than likely, she lacks genuine praise in her life, which is why she doesn't mind seeking it from men in the gym. It makes my heart hurt to think that someone may be relying solely on that type of feedback. We cannot judge. What we need to do is seek to understand the why.

After all, I would never judge my daughter for wanting my attention. It's a healthy craving. The problem is that desire can produce some extremely unhealthy tactics when we don't feel like we are getting it. That is when something normal and natural to crave becomes a driving force behind all of the little decisions we make. It can also end up driving the things that you do and say negatively. It can also drive you to a place of compromise because as long as it produces the result of getting the attention, it's worth it. Even if that attention is negative, it is still, to the attention seeker, better than no attention at all.

Unfortunately, we live in a world where people's attention is divided and usually amongst things that hold no eternal value. This leaves things that matter in the long term starved for your attention and affection. In a society where people's jobs kept them distracted from giving their children the attention they wanted, now add entertainment in the form of your handheld device. Children are no longer getting the attention that they need.

So that drive to get attention, I believe, is at an all-time high. I haven't even mentioned people that were missing a parent altogether. I fall in that category. My father wasn't around, so the attention that a little girl gets typically from her father wasn't just lacking but entirely missing.

Whether your story is that your parents were absent or

absent-minded, it can still produce the same result. Neediness begins to arise in you. I have got to do something or be something that gets the attention that I have lacked in life.

Some children can find positive outlets to pour their time and energy into to get the attention they desire for being the best at playing their instrument or their sport. But like myself, some cannot afford to pursue such things. They are leaving you to either get very creative or pour yourself into an obvious place where attention seems to come quickly.

In my case, this was boys. I always preferred my friends that were boys. My best friends were always boys, which quickly turned into boyfriends because I would agree to be their girlfriend, not to hurt my best friend's feelings. Eventually, it would get weird, and then I would no longer have my friend. And that was a pattern that happened so many times before I finally realized that I could if I wanted to get attention from boys because, for whatever reason, they liked me. I was a tomboy growing up, so I didn't realize that boys thought I was pretty until I was in like 8th grade. But even after that, I felt like it was more about my recent developments.

But because I was always naturally more comfortable around boys, it made them feel more comfortable and natural, and I guess they just didn't have that same ease with other girls. Once I finally understood this dynamic, I used it to my advantage. Even when I didn't pursue a relationship for attention, I still almost always had a sidekick. It would be my boy best friend that would give me all of the attention that I needed while pretending that he wasn't, in fact, in love with me because it would ruin our friendship.

I have had times of regret thinking back to friendships that were entirely about me. I even found out some huge things about one of my best friends years later, and I was filled with guilt because I never knew and never asked.

When you live your life to get all of the attention you crave, you become a very shallow and selfish person. Every decision you make is wrapped around the type of response that you will get. I traded my best friends that I had invested a few years into for the popular girls in the middle of 8th grade solely because of the attention that it would generate. In those moments, I was trading the real and the genuine for the fake and superficial, but I was willing to because I would be popular.

It is quite challenging to have a meaningful relationship with another person when the only thing that matters to you within that friendship is how that person can serve you. When all that matters is how well they listen to you and how well they cater to the type of relationship you are looking for.

Attention-seeking leaves you lonely and no better off than you were before. Every high you get from attention almost always leaves you empty or regretful because you aren't true to yourself. Most likely, along the way, you had to compromise things you believe in because they gave the attention wanted.

I came to the point where I was sick and tired of living off of boys' attention. It left all of the relationships I had with women strained, and it produced no result. Everything I did was all about manipulation and how that person could make me feel. I then tried pursuing the unexpected, like the one's way outside of my social sphere, because they would respond with feeling unworthy of my attention. I let the pursuers come after me because of the way that their begging made me feel. I tried getting attention from the good guy, the bad guy, the reckless guy, the one in need, the new guy, you name it. At the end of the day, I was still alone, empty, and in need.

I had been taught how to pursue God, but I never made it a priority because I was consumed with the game that I was playing. I cannot be more thankful for the timing when God just took over. He put me around the positive association, inserted mentors in my life, and began to show me a different path. Had I taken the patterns I was living in into my adult life, I am terrified to think of what that would have produced. I was pursuing modeling because It was the career that I would get the most attention.

But God gave me a vision for something that would matter, something that would make a difference in other people's lives, and I had just enough good left in me, and I was still so much in need, so I let go of that life.

I decided that I would spend the rest of my life pursuing God and the plan that he had for me, and I didn't care how long it would take to produce a result I was willing to. I invested my free time into my future and sought God so that he might repair my heart that was shattered. I stop spending time with the people that I only hung around once again because of the type of attention they gave me. I began to trade stupid weekend adventures of making one wrong decision after another in for quiet nights spending time with God. Writing, praying, and reading his word.

It was tempting to go back into that life, especially when it got a bit lonely. But it wasn't long until I began to realize why I was craving attention so badly. I began to feel like God was responding to me seeking him. I felt him coming closer and closer to me, and the thought of him leaning into me just made my heart swell. It was easy then for me to see that all I needed was God and his attention.

Not seeking attention allowed me to make healthier

decisions in my life. I was no longer in need of that superficial high, so that made my standards higher. It wasn't until I met a man seeking God as fervently as I was that I began to crave something other than God alone. I felt ok with this desire, though, because I knew that God was the one putting him in my path. He loved God and needed God more than he needed me, and he was clear about that from the beginning. We promised that we would never distract each other from our relationships with God, leaving him jealous and in need of our attention. We decided that we would always push each other towards our creator.

In times where either one of us has been in need, we have reminded each other of the only one that can provide all it is that we need.

You may be thinking, If I had someone in my life like that, I wouldn't spend so much of my time seeking attention. And that may be true, but had I not stopped living my life in the way I was, I would have missed my opportunity to have him. God wouldn't have brought us together because he trusted us, and even if we had accidentally run into each other, there would have been nothing to draw us together. The one thing that made us stand out to each other was that we were not seeking attention. We were seeking God.

I am not going to lie to you and tell you it will be easy. At first, it will be very hard. It will be an entire lifestyle shift. But it will be a cleanse of all of the things in your life that don't matter. You will have more time and energy to find something you can be passionate about and excel in. You will have a real and tangible relationship with the one that created you, and through that relationship, you are likely to realize what he created you for. There is no better attention than your father applauding you for doing what only you can do best. Don't you want to know what that might be?

Psalm 119:10: With my whole heart, I seek you.

When we seek God above all other things, we experience real fulfillment and validation. There is nothing else that can give you that.

Journal

In what areas of your life have you sought recognition or attention from others?

Did you or do you recognize anything you currently do as a form of attention-seeking?

Action Steps

Be intentional about spending time with God! Practice today truly seeking him before other things. Before you open social media on your phone, or before you turn on the tv or radio. Pause and take the time to seek God.

Prayer

Dear heavenly Father, help me right now, and at this moment, be aware of the things I do for attention. Help me to see those things and the results that that behavior has produced. Purify my heart and my intentions right now, God. Help me begin thinking and doing not for getting others to pay attention to me but for the result of capturing your attention and affection. I want to seek your face, father, and I want to know your will for my life. Bring me quick conviction when I begin slipping down that path and bring me closer to you, God. I desire to please you and bring you glory and fame and care only about what you want for my life.

25

SELF-NEGLECT

Self-Care is building a strategy to defeat self-neglect.

Don't just be good to others, be good to you!

I know that this is a topic that is often covered these days. I just feel like I wanted to join in and maybe add to the conversation. Everyone talks about self-care and its importance. Right now, at this very moment, I am on a little self-care staycation. I picked a beautiful hotel in my city with the best jacuzzi tubs in their rooms and booked a spot. I wanted to be able to get away, unwind, unplug and finish up this book.

I am a wife, a mother, a business owner, a loyal friend. I am trying to be an accomplished writer (I guess I will figure out how that's working for me) and so much more. Women wear so many different hats, and we are such caregivers to others and not nearly enough to ourselves.

You cannot pour from an empty kettle. If you are empty, tired, worn down, and unwell, no matter how hard you try, you are not going to be able to give all that you want to others. You must pour into yourself to pour out.

So yes, start trying some new things and find out some of the self-care things that seem the most beneficial to you.

You can go on walks, run, take long baths or showers, treat yourself to frequent massages, make time just to sit and think, make time to read or meditate, take yourself on a date. The list is endless, and everyone has their thing that they enjoy the most.

My question to you because I am the annoying little kid that always asks WHY.

Is just that, why have you been neglecting yourself?

Sometimes the answer to this is simple. I just have gotten caught up with the busyness of life, and I have put myself last. Everyone does it at one point or another. I am not necessarily saying you will always be able to put yourself first, especially if you have children. Just don't completely ignore yourself and your needs altogether. Be intentional about making sure you do something for yourself every once in a while.

Then there are those of you out there who had reason to believe that they were no good, worthless trash. So it was intentional. You stopped taking care of yourself because whatever happened to you or in your life made you feel like it wasn't worth it anymore. You stopped. No one noticed, so maybe it just fortified in your mind that it didn't matter.

Some women have been so degraded, whether it was physically, mentally, or emotionally that the concept of self-care doesn't even make sense. When you have been told that no one cares about you, whether through deeds or words, why would you care about yourself? Or maybe through sexual abuse, you have decided that neglect was the best way to make sure that you were no longer attractive to the person who has victimized you. You have not invested in yourself for so long because of what happened that it is just a normal thing for you. It seems to not bother anyone else, so you just let it go. The truth is this could quite possibly be one of the most challenging topics ever to bring up to someone. Especially for the people that genuinely love you because that means they probably know your story and why you have made that choice. Maybe you have even allowed sympathy from others to fuel your decision to get to this place where you almost act as if you are the trash that others made you feel you were.

Some women have experienced such tragedy that it was understandable to be in a slump for a season. Maybe you feel like it would be selfish or insensitive to take care of yourself in light of such loss and pain. I think for a time, it may even seem inappropriate to others if you "take care of yourself." People almost expect the worst from people amidst significant loss. It would be socially acceptable for you to crawl into a ball and freak out. The problem is that the people that would judge you for not grieving appropriately will also judge you for not "getting it together" after so long. You have permission to go through a grieving process when you have met loss. I am saying that it is normal, but it is tricky because you wonder when it is ok for me to be me again. You ask yourself when you can smile again, laugh again, do everyday things again without feeling guilty.

When we lose things, we almost tend to feel like we owe something of ourselves for that, and the truth is we don't. Everyone experiences loss and grieves in their way, but the key is to get back up. It doesn't serve anyone for you or help your case to live in that dark place now for the rest of your days. Loss is a part of life, and if it were meant to ruin us, then God would never again ask anything of us, but you already know that he still wants you to do what he sent you out to do. That could be why you are still reading this book.

The truth is that no matter what happened that caused you to neglect yourself, you must understand that you are now making God suffer the consequences. He has given you your life to be a temple and a vessel for the holy spirit. When you neglect it, you neglect him. When you don't take care of your body, you limit what God can do through you. When you don't feed your spirit man, he will starve, and then how is God supposed to do anything with that?

Darling Woman, you are a creation of God. He doesn't make junk. He wouldn't have wasted time making you if he didn't have a purpose for you. The fact that you are alive is proof that you have a purpose. If you feel right now that maybe you would start caring about yourself if you had a calling, but you haven't found what that is yet, so you have nothing to fight for. Let me just tell you that if you don't know yet, but you are willing to step out and take care of the one thing that is yours alone to take care of. Along the way, he will begin to plant passions inside of you. If you start to take steps into self-care and maybe nothing fits, but you're willing to try a few things, something will. Chances are, whatever it is that he uses to heal you and begin to enhance you is something you will become passionate about, and in turn, he will use you through that to heal and improve the lives of others.

If you think you are good at taking care of others while ignoring yourself, imagine what you can do for others when fueled with passion and strength.

1 Corinthians 6:19-20: Do you not know that your bodies are temples of the Holy Spirit, who is in you, whom you have received from God? You are not your own; you were bought at a price. Therefore honor God with your bodies.

If what I have said so far has not convinced you, then let me just remind you that Jesus died to buy your life. He must have seen the immense value in you when he chose to trade his life so that you might live free of the curse of sin and death. So I guess all that is left to say is are you living your life currently in a way that is worthy of that sacrifice. It is not just about working for others. It is also very much about taking care of yourself because he died for you just as much as he died for the ones you ignore yourself to serve. You belong to him. How do you think he wants his precious one treated?

Sis, It is time to stop ignoring yourself. Take the step into showing yourself some love, and God will show up for the journey to love you too.

Journal

Do you feel like you neglect yourself, and if so, do you know why?

If you are ready to change this area, what are you going to try first?

Action Steps

- Make a list of ways that you are going to be intentional about taking care of yourself this week AND DO IT!

Prayer

God, I just want to thank you for the life that you have given me. Help me not take my life for granted and heal me of the things that have caused me to neglect myself. I need your love and affection above all, but I also need your strength so that I can take care of this vessel you have entrusted to me. I have a strong desire to do great things for you, God, so I just ask that you show me how to best take care of myself to become the person you created me to be. I know that you don't make junk, so I declare from this moment on I will treat myself the way you would want me treated, and I know you will do the rest.

26

NARCISSISM

Narcissism: excessive interest in or admiration of oneself and one's physical appearance.

Darling, here is the deal, and if you are narcissistic, there is absolutely no way you will think this is about you. So maybe just pause for a second and ask for God to reveal to you if this is an area in which you struggle. Narcissistic people tend to think that everything is about them for sure but never the bad things. They are also very rarely wrong. They dominate environments and exercise this false control in all of their relationships.

Narcissism is so challenging to be around because, in any environment, it is unbelievably overpowering.

You may be narcissistic if you get together with someone and the entire time is spent talking about you. If you didn't ask the person you spent time with any questions about themselves and you just talked the whole time, that is a pretty good indicator. Conversations are supposed to go both ways, and if they just learned all about your life and your drama and knew nothing about them, you were behaving narcissistically.

These people brag about themselves and their accomplishments all of the time to make people think that they are successful, and maybe they are, but they need you to know it and be in awe of them. They also want attention for it. They want attention for being strong, so sometimes they are a bit premature in giving details in negative and private situations so that everyone will be shocked by how they can handle themselves. They want you to know what they are going through to build themselves up on your comments on how brave they are.

The only topic of conversation is them.

I know some women like this, and I just have to stay away from them. I don't want to come off as super judgmental. The fact of the matter is that my dad is extremely narcissistic, and that has left such a bad taste in my mouth that I just cannot stand anything that remotely resembles it. If you have a conversation with him, it is about him. If you tell him that he has hurt you, he tells you how it is your fault or his dad's fault for the way he treated him as a child. I am no therapist, and I am not claiming to be. I hope that you haven't gotten that impression from this book. I am just talking openly about things that I have dealt with. I am sure there is a much more in-depth explanation for all of this, but this is just how I think.

The biggest thing is that narcissistic people are selfish, and that affects all of their relationships. They live their lives like they are putting on a show, and they want people who are attentive to that show and give them a round of applause and standing ovation on the appropriate ques. If you don't provide them with the attention that they need, you will not be a priority in their life. There is just one fundamental problem with that way of life. You are not that important. You are not more important than everyone in your life regardless of how much you know, how educated or successful you are. So don't pretend to be, and don't force the people in your life into that position. Short term, you may like audience members as your friends, but they will get sick and tired of watching the same old show long-term.

If you fear this may be you honestly, it will take time and effort to reverse this way of life, but the steps to get better are simple. If you take a few simple steps to be more inclusive, then the people in your life will notice right away, and trust me, they will appreciate it.

1. Check-in on people, you probably have many people who reach out to you, but they never get the same in return. SEND THEM A TEXT!

2. If you are in a conversation, pay attention to how much you are talking. If you are doing all the talking, slow down and say, "what's new with you."

3. Try not bragging about anything for a week, depending on how hard that is. It can be a pretty good indicator of how often you were doing this before and how big of a problem it may be.

4. Talk to God about this, what has caused you to be selfish and self-promoting. I know it seems like I am harsh, but I am almost sure that it is not your fault.

I feel like narcissism can be the root of some serious issues in your life and relationships. Healthy relationships require a certain amount of selflessness, which is difficult for someone narcissistic, so their relationships suffer. Some people don't understand why they have challenges in all of their relationships, and they have never thought long enough to realize they are the common denominator. I believe that if someone is narcissistic, there are deeper root issues at play. I feel like there is a need to dive deeper with God into what those roots could be.

Journal

Do you think this is you?

Are you willing to let God take you on a deeper journey?

Ask him why Am I like this God. Can you help me?

Action Steps

Follow the challenge list above of ways to be more inclusive and take notes on your experience.

Prayer

God, I feel like narcissism has been an issue in my life, and it has affected my friendships and my close and personal relationships. I don't want to be that person that seems completely self-obsessed because I am interested in the people around me, and I want better relationships. So God, at this moment, right now, I turn to you for validation, I turn to you for the attention that I seek, and I refuse to request it from others anymore. You are all I need. I will refocus myself on you. Help me invest more into others and be a person that other people come to when they need someone to listen. Only you can rewire me, and I need to be rewired, Jesus.

27

UNHEALTHY FOOD RELATIONSHIPS

"Our food should be our medicine and our medicine should
be our food." —Hippocrates

Oh boy, this is a tough one. If you struggle in this area or
even to the extreme of having had dealt with an eating
disorder, or you still are now, this is a chapter that you probably
want to skip. I just didn't want to skip anything that I know I
could speak just a little bit too. I like to tell people that
experience is useful when talking about tough topics like this.
Ultimately people have a hard time receiving help from people
who have never been in their shoes.

Admittedly I have never dealt with an eating disorder
personally. I have someone very close to me who has, but that
still does not make me an expert. I don't know all of the
intricacies and the battles she faced daily while in the thick of it,
and I don't know fully what it felt like for her to get well.

I know that once you are healthy and you have overcome

your eating disorder, it is still something that can affect your life. You have to be intentional not to slip into old patterns.

My friend, I would like to tell you that if you struggle with an eating disorder that you absolutely can get your life back, you can get better, and you can have a normal relationship with food again in the future if that is something you desire. You may not care enough, but the people around you do. They want and need you to get better. I can tell you from experience that what they see in you is so far from what you see in yourself. You are far more beautiful than you realize. God wants you to be happy, healthy and see yourself the way he sees you.

I am sorry I cannot offer more than a suggestion to seek help. Find someone you can talk to as a start. If you have never told anyone, that is probably a good first step. Try seeking a pastor or someone you know you can trust to be delicate. Many counselors out there specialize in dealing with women who are plagued by an eating disorder. I am sure there will be a lot of work involved, but you are worth it.

For me, the unhealthy relationship I had with food had way more to deal with why I chose to eat at any given time. I ate when I was hungry like everyone else. I ate when something looked or smelled good. I ate when I was bored. I ate when I was sad and needed comfort. I snacked when I watched television.

Growing up, there were so many times when our dinners were eating in front of the tv while " our shows" were on. As an adult, If I was sitting in front of a tv, then food should be eaten. It was a pattern in my life that I had developed.

I saw very little consequence for this lifestyle until about my mid-twenties, when I began to put on a little weight. Then I just decided to make working out a very consistent part of my life, and because I made that shift, I was able to keep up with the eating patterns that I was used to. It wasn't until after I had my daughter via c-section that my entire body composition completely changed. Working out was more difficult, but it just came down to how I ate in the past was no longer going to be a sustainable lifestyle if I didn't want to put on a significant amount of weight. The problem was not just that I was always hungry and had such a crazy metabolism. It was the fact that eating was associated with more things than it needed to be. If I can be extreme, eating was put so high in my life that it felt like happiness. So it was quite often a pretty quick fix to a lot of issues in my life. Once I started seeing the consequences show up on my body, I was motivated to think about the way I ate.

I am now a mother, and I want to pass down healthy eating habits to my daughter. I want her to grow up to understand one simple thing, food is fuel. This fact is exceptionally annoying, but if you are put in a position where you have to fight to survive, food becomes something you think differently. It is not something you indulge in but something you need to live. Truly that is what it is designed for. Food gives us the energy we need to carry out our daily tasks. Food is supposed to keep us healthy and strong. But most people see food as one of the biggest things in their life.

I will admit I am a foodie. Especially when I am traveling, I love to try new places and try fresh foods. But when that is a way of life, you will suffer more consequences than you realize. You make decisions based on extremely short-term pleasure rather than on long-term health. Think about it when you eat something, its taste lasts only as long as it is on your tongue, but once you swallow it, that taste is gone. If you are making poor food choices, that bad food is sitting in your stomach, affecting your body for much longer than it was on your tongue. The risk seems to outweigh the reward in this situation.

We can make some very short-term decisions when it comes

to the food that we eat. Here is the thing, I am not telling you that you should start eating like a bird or that you should never indulge. If you run to food for pleasure, satisfaction, fulfillment, comfort, or any other reason, you need to recognize that pattern. I am not saying you can never have dessert again, I couldn't handle that type of restriction.

I am saying indulge but don't make indulging a part of your lifestyle. I believe we are called to live long and healthy lives, and we aren't helping in that if we cannot control the way we eat.

1 Corinthians 10:31: So whether you eat or drink or whatever you do, do it all for the glory of God.

If you have abided by this scripture already in your life, you are just flat out a better person than me. I have never eaten A meal in my life, thinking I am doing this to glorify you. I don't believe so many are, and I don't believe that God is upset with me about it. But I know that it is a simple adjustment to use food as fuel, and if you do that, you will be fueled up to fulfill the callings God has on your life.

This chapter is simple, but hopefully, it can help you think about your habits and food patterns. I am convicted, especially after reading this scripture. Our whole lives are for him. There is no area of our life that he is not interested in. I know it probably seems exhausting to have all of these things to pay attention to, but it takes minimal effort to just be intentional with your eating.

You can say it is not a big deal all you want, but if your body is making you unhappy or you are binge eating, and it causes you sadness, you need to get a grip on it. The important thing that I want you to know is that you are not alone. Unhealthy relationships with food are more common than you realize. Don't feel defeated because you lack self-control. This is an area where I felt like I had no control at points, but you can get that back.

I am not talking about some weight loss or fad diet. I am talking about choosing what you eat based on what it does for your body rather than what it tastes like on your tongue. And not always, but the sweets are much sweeter when they are a treat for a disciplined lifestyle.

I am currently teaching myself that desserts are rewards, not daily, right.

Journal

Do you feel like you have an unhealthy relationship with food?

If so, in what way?

What are the first steps you plan to take with your eating habits?

What is your Goal with these steps?

Action Steps

- Do some research on superfoods and add something new to your diet this week to fuel you.

Prayer

God, I have no desire to be controlled by anything but you. I do not want to live solely to gratify my flesh, and I don't want my relationship with food to be so out of whack any longer. I want to use everything you give me for its original intention, and food is one of them. Help me, God, help the way I think about food and strengthen me to have self-control. I am thankful for my health and life, and I do not want to take unnecessary risks. Help me to have wisdom in the way that I eat Jesus. I dedicate this new area of my life to you. (Unless I am Pregnant, God, then just give me grace and a hedge of protection for ten months). I will have healthy eating patterns, and I will teach them to my children so that we may be better examples for you.

Amen.

28

SELF DOUBT

"It's not who you are that holds you back: it's what you think you are not." —Anonymous

Self-doubt is the enemy of the creative. It is the enemy to your future and to the plans that God has promised you. It is the enemy to the life that you know that you deserve.

There is humility, and then there is self-doubt, and those are two entirely different things, darling.

The most dangerous part of self-doubt is that it is not just about you. Self-doubt gets you in the nasty habit of denying the power of God within you. You hide away the gifts that God gave you to bring him glory, and you do that all because you don't feel good enough.

This is the harsh truth. It is not about you.

Do you know how many writers there are in the world, my friend? Do you know how many people have written a book? I have to keep myself encouraged because this is an extremely daunting fact to anyone who feels they have been called to write. Do you know how easy it is to doubt myself and my writing ability? Or how easy it is to say, I may be good, but so and so is better, and they have already covered this topic, so you know what, I am just going to go ahead and let them keep killing it.

It is challenging to push yourself forward into something when you don't feel like you are enough and don't feel worthy.

Here are some hard truths.

You are worthy of God's love but not his glory, so if God raises you to the point where men give you credit, it is entirely for the ability to point it back to him. This should release pressure from you. I do not write to be GREAT. I write to be effective and to know that I am helping someone feel the closeness to God that I have felt. I am not worthy of success because I have been gifted the ability to form words into a book. So whatever happens, it is not about you!

You are not good enough.

Woah, Paige, I thought this book was to help women, that is not helping. Here is the thing doll-face, you are terrific, like seriously, you are epic. But to accomplish all of the things you know you are supposed to, you are not good enough. You need other people, and you need God. Nothing gained alone is worth having because you have no one to enjoy it with.

Moses gained freedom for an entire people, but he had the power of God working on his behalf the whole time. He also had people who believed in him and believed in his message enough to follow him. The people that followed first started a trend, and then when they gained their independence from the Egyptian people, they all celebrated together because it was a win for the people, for Moses. Most importantly, it was a win for God. The only thing that stood in the way of those very people making it into the land of promise was doubt.

Now bear with me here, it is ridiculously Disney, but it is unbelievably true.

> "There can be miracles when you believe.
> Though Hope is frail, it's hard to kill.
> Who knows what miracles you can achieve?
> When you believe, somehow you will."

This beautiful song plays in the Disney movie *The Prince Of Egypt*.

And it is sung by Mariah Carey and Whitney Houston. It is capable of breaking me all the way down to tears in just seconds because it has such a powerful message.

You can achieve things by mastering a craft and honing a skill, but you achieve miracles by believing. When you have been given a mission, it is easy first to question why you were the one chosen. Just as Moses did, he had all sorts of doubts and fears. If you have a mission that God has asked you to accomplish that you have had a very similar conversation to the one Moses had with God, here is how it went down.

By the way, I am paraphrasing all of this.

Exodus 3-4: God: I have seen the suffering of my people in Egypt, and I am sending you to set them free.

Moses: Who Am I that I should go?

God: I will be going with you

Moses: What if I go and they ask me, "Who sent you," what do I say then?

God: "I AM WHO I AM"... I AM has sent me to you.

This is my name forever, the name you should call me from generation to generation

Moses: What if they don't believe me and tell me that I never had his conversation with you?

God: What's in your hand?

Moses: A staff

God: Throw it on the ground

Moses: Throws said, staff

God: Turns said staff into a snake, scares Moses, tells him to pick it up, and say, this is how I will show them that I am with you, and we did have this conversation.

Moses: Ok, but I don't speak well in front of people. I am slow in speech and tongue.

God: Who gave you your mouth?

Moses: uhhhhhh

God: GO, and I will speak through you and tell you what to say

Wow, how awesome is that? What is crazy is that Exodus 4:12, the last line in the conversation from up above, is one of my favorite scriptures. I like to speak this any time before I am about to speak in front of people. I want to initiate that reliance on him not to feel like I have to impress or perform but instead just be a vessel. But what is so funny is that when I look at the rest of that conversation, I realized I have had that same talk with God so often.

You think standing right there in the presence of God, you would just agree to whatever it is he was saying to you. Moses had a lot of courage to speak his doubts and wasn't punished for them either because he is human. So just know that it is a natural reaction to a lofty goal given to you by your father. The whole point is that God is sending you because it defeats his purpose to do it himself. He gets the glory from using imperfect people like you and me. He needs us to be His vessels, and through us, he will get it accomplished.

When God tells me to write because there are things that

women need to hear, I need to realize that he hasn't chosen me because of how good I am but because of how willing I am. This is an excellent way not only to check your pride but also to keep you out of doubt. It is not about your capabilities but the fact that he can use you to get things accomplished.

I talk so much about Moses, but one of the most disappointing things is that he never made it to the promised land. He was obedient to the call on his life but dealt with just enough doubt that he wouldn't follow instructions thoroughly. On the other hand, Joshua had no doubt, which is why he made it to the promised land. Someone will come along where you have been paused by doubt, and they will fulfill the mission. There is an example of this in Esther.

Esther 4:14: For if you remain silent at this time, relief and deliverance for the Jews will arise from another place, but you and your father's family will perish. And who knows but that you have come to your royal position for such a time as this?"

Most people take the ladder part of this scripture out of context to encourage. It is almost always used as a call to action. But in context, it was something to be taken into careful consideration. I see it as a warning. Think about it. Maybe you were born for this very moment, not to doubt what God has told you to do. Not to ask questions or worry about the outcome but to act in holy obedience. You just have to do it. If you think about it, too much fear will overcome you, and you will question whether you should or not. Esther was called to do something punishable by death which was why this scripture was not to empower her. It was to tell her that regardless of if she took action or not, there is still the threat of death. But what if she dies, having never done the one thing that she was born for.

Regardless of what God needs to be done will be done. If you don't do it, someone else will, and then you die without having ever fulfilled the one thing you were created for, which is more frightening to me than anything man could ever do to me.

So I refuse to let myself get in the way by living in doubt, and I think it is time for you to stop doubting too.

Journal

What has God asked you to do with your life that intimidates you?

What are the doubts that have arisen in your mind?

Do you believe that God can overcome your limitations?

Action Steps

Write out all of the doubts you have that keep you from doing what you know you are called to do. Pray through each doubt and ask God to be strong where you are weak and make up for what you lack. Then take action on what you have been hesitating in.

Prayer

Here I am, God, just like Moses, and I believe that I have heard you tell me things that you have wanted me to do. In the moment of hearing an assignment, the first thing I thought about was my limitations rather than the fact that the one who sent me is greater than any of that. I ask right now to reignite that conversation within me again, God. I want you to send me wherever you would have me go, trusting not just in the fact that you have equipped me but in the fact that you will be with me. I want to come to that place, God, to where I can step out, knowing this is the moment for which I was created. I want to live in that type of obedience.

29

CONCLUSION

Friend, I am so unbelievably thankful and humbled that you decided to come along on this journey with me. I hope that it helped you to read it as much as it challenged me and helped me to write it. I know there were probably many moments when you were like, dang, this girl has some issues, but here is the thing, so did you. We can either hide them, run from them, or embrace them and do the work it takes to change. To become the women, we long to be.

We are never going to arrive at this place where we are perfect. But we can receive 100% healing, and we can overcome and conquer our strongholds. Most importantly, we can be the best gardener in the neighborhood by pulling on our gloves and getting to work and not just trimming the weeds at the top, spraying weed eater, and moving on but by uprooting those bad boys. If God did not plant it in you, then it doesn't have the power to remain when you begin to pull with the power and authority of Christ. I just believe that every single thing that entangled you before is now loose and uprooted. I am hoping that you have begun to realize that you are not alone in your struggles and the whole purpose that he has walked me through any of these issues was for you.

I had no idea why I always had to face the hard things I faced, but I promise you to know now that it was meant to help make your life better. I would go through it all again. It just would have been nice to be able to picture your pretty face as a reminder of why it was essential to pick me up from the mud. You are worth it, and I hope you know that.

Nothing in your life needs to remain now but the beautiful things that bear fruit and pretty flowers.

I Love you, my dear friend, and I am excited for this new season of freedom in your life.

Can we pray together one last time?

Final Prayer

Dear Heavenly Father,

Thank you so much for these sweet sisters of mine that have decided to come along on this journey with me. I have covered some in-depth topics here, and we have all worked together to uproot some things. God, I just pray that for every void created from every uprooted issue, I pray that you fill that space with your presence. I speak wholeness in this one's life. And if there was some pain in the process of uprooting that you continue to bring healing. That although this book is done, your work is not. Even if I develop a green thumb, you are the ultimate gardener and the only one that can bring their healing to completion, so I ask for completion right now.

Thank you for this opportunity to use some of my life issues as a testimony to help others and remind my new friend that nothing she went through was in vain, but so your power could overcome everything, and she could also be a testimony of your goodness.

Thank you for this time, this fellowship, and I ask that these truths take root, in your name Jesus.

Amen.

ABOUT THE AUTHOR

Paige Loehr lives in Overland Park, Kansas with her husband and two children. They have been business owners for over a decade and have been able to focus their lifestyle around their family. A relationship with God is the center of Paige's life, and because of that, she has encountered healing in many areas. So, it is her joy to share that healing with others. Paige is passionate about helping people feel the freedom that she lives in every single day.

Made in the USA
Columbia, SC
11 April 2021